FIRST NATIONAL EDITION

TAKING CARE

OF YOUR

CORPORATION

Volume 1:
Shareholder and Director
Meetings Made Easy

BY ATTORNEY ANTHONY MANCUSO

EDITED BY RALPH WARNER & LISA GOLDOFTAS

NOLO PRESS   BERKELEY

YOUR RESPONSIBILITY WHEN USING A SELF-HELP LAW BOOK

We've done our best to give you useful and accurate information in this book. But laws and procedures change frequently and are subject to differing interpretations. If you want legal advice backed by a guarantee, see a lawyer. If you use this book, it's your responsibility to make sure that the facts and general advice contained in it are applicable to your situation.

KEEPING UP-TO-DATE

To keep its books up-to-date, Nolo Press issues new printings and new editions periodically. New printings reflect minor legal changes and technical corrections. New editions contain major legal changes, major text additions or major reorganizations. To find out if a later printing or edition of any Nolo book is available, call Nolo Press at (510) 549-1976 or check the catalog in the Nolo News, our quarterly newspaper.

To stay current, follow the "Update" service in the Nolo News. You can get the paper free by sending us the registration card in the back of the book. In another effort to help you use Nolo's latest materials, we offer a 25% discount off the purchase of any new Nolo book if you turn in any earlier printing or edition. (See the "Recycle Offer" in the back of the book.)

This book was last revised in: JULY 1994.

First Edition	JULY 1994
Editors	RALPH WARNER & LISA GOLDOFTAS
Illustrations	MARI STEIN
Cover Design	TONI IHARA
Book Design	JACKIE MANCUSO
Proofreading	ELY NEUMAN
Index	MARY KIDD
Printing	DELTA LITHOGRAPH

Mancuso, Anthony
    Taking care of your corporation / by Anthony Mancuso. -- 1st national ed.
        p.   cm.
    Includes index.
    ISBN 0-87337-223-9
    1. Corporation law--United States--Popular works. e
governance--United States--Popular works. 3. Industrial management-
-United States--Popular works. I. Title.
KF1416.M36 1994
346.73'066--dc20
[347.30666]   94-2649
                                                                 CIP

recycled paper

ACKNOWLEDGEMENTS

Many thanks to Lisa Goldoftas for a superb job of eding and clarifying material for final production copy, and to Jake Warner for tackling the first umpteen passes through this book and enormously helpful ideas. Thanks also to Jackie and Toni for their great design and production work.

iii

TABLE OF CONTENTS

Introduction

CHAPTER 1

Corporate Documents and Laws

CHAPTER 4

How to Hold a Meeting of Your Directors or Shareholders

CHAPTER 5

How to Prepare Written Minutes of Shareholders Meetings

CHAPTER 10

Computer User's Guide

APPENDIX A

Corporate Filing Offices

APPENDIX B

State Business Corporation Statutes

APPENDIX C

Tear-Out Corporate Records Forms

INTRODUCTION

This book is designed to help relatively small, privately-held corporations do their own corporate legal housekeeping efficiently and at low cost. To this end, the book shows you step-by-step how to comply with legal formalities required of all corporations:

- hold and document corporate meetings of shareholders and directors, and

- document corporate action taken without a meeting.

The paperwork used to provide this documentation consists of minutes and written consent forms for shareholders and directors. To help you complete these forms, we have included detailed instructions and sample forms. All forms are included in Appendix C and on the corporate records disk accompanying this book.

The information and forms in this book are intended for smaller incorporated businesses. By "smaller," we mean those that are privately-owned (stock is not offered and sold to the public) with a manageable number of shareholders (up to about 35) and employees (up to about 50). A typical example is a family-owned business or one in which all stock is owned by several people. Similarly, this book is primarily directed toward businesses in which the people who own a significant amount of stock are actively involved in managing, or at least supervising, the business or have a close personal or pre-existing business relationship with those who perform these tasks. Businesses in this category typically have annual sales from $100,000 to $10,000,000.

Another way to make this point is to say that the material here is primarily intended for directors and shareholders who have a substantial degree of commonalty of interest and vision for their smaller-sized corporation—people who routinely work together and can attend to necessary corporate procedures and recordkeeping without a great deal of controversy.

The Reason for This Book

Forming a corporation is an important, and sometimes exhausting, task. Typically, after the new entity is established and the initial shares sold to stockholders, the owners take a deep breath and get back to doing what they do best—running the day-to-day business operations. As a result, the owners often put off dealing with the many tasks necessary to properly run their new corporate entity.

Leaving the care and feeding of your corporate legal entity undone is foolhardy. Failure to properly document and support important tax decisions and elections can result in a loss of crucial tax benefits. Even worse, the fact that you have ignored your own corporate existence may result in its being similarly disregarded by the courts, with the risk that you may be held personally liable for corporate debts.

Or, to put all of this more positively, your first and best line of defense against losing the protection of your corporate status is to treat your corporation with respect. Above all, this means documenting important corporate decisions by preparing and maintaining adequate corporate records. With the help of this book, you can do most of this routine paperwork yourself, turning to a lawyer or accountant only when you need help with a complicated legal or tax issue.

Why Key Corporate Decisions Should Be Recorded

The good news is that you don't need to make or document most business decisions—only those that require formal board of director or shareholder approval. In other words, it's not required by law or practice that you clutter up your corporate records book with mundane business records about purchasing supplies or products, hiring or firing employees, deciding to launch new services or products, or any of the host of other ongoing business decisions.

But key legal, tax and financial decisions absolutely should be acted on by your board of directors, and occasionally your shareholders. What kinds of decisions are considered "key"? The proceedings of annual meetings of directors and shareholders, the issuance of stock to new or existing shareholders, the purchase of real property, the authorization of a significant loan amount or substantial line of credit, and the making of important federal or state tax elections. These, and other key decisions, should be made by your board of directors or shareholders and backed with corporate paperwork. That way, you'll have solid documentation in the event key decisions are questioned or reviewed later by corporate directors, shareholders, creditors, the courts or the IRS.

There's more good news about the task ahead of you. As you'll learn, having your board of directors ratify important corporate decisions doesn't necessarily mean dragging directors to a formal meeting, although this is one option. Corporate decisions can also legally be made over the phone, by mail, fax machine, computer e-mail or bulletin board conference, or any other practical means of communication among directors or shareholders. And once decisions are made, there are several easy-to-use ways to document these decisions—by preparing written minutes for a corporate meeting or preparing written consent forms signed by the directors or shareholders.[1] If the consent form method is used, no meeting is held; instead, directors sign a form that shows agreement to a particular transaction or decision.

Why bother to prepare minutes of meetings or written consents for important corporate decisions? Here are a few excellent reasons:

- Annual corporate meetings are required under state law. If you fail to pay at least minimal attention to these ongoing legal formalities, you may lose the protection of your corporate status.

- As time passes and memories fade, your legal paperwork provides a record of important corporate transactions. This "paper trail" can be important if disputes arise. You can use this paper trail to show your directors, shareholders, creditors, suppliers, the IRS and the courts that you acted appropriately and in compliance with applicable laws, regulations or other legal requirements.

- Formally documenting key corporate action is a fail-proof way of keeping shareholders informed of major corporate decisions.

- Directors of small corporations commonly approve business transactions in which they have a material financial interest. Your minutes or consent forms can help prevent legal problems by proving that these self-interested decisions were arrived at fairly, after full disclosure to the board and shareholders.

---

[1]Most states allow any action that can be taken at a meeting to be taken by written consent of directors or shareholders—see Chapter 7.

- Banks, trust, escrow and title companies, property management companies and other institutions often ask corporations to submit a copy of a board or shareholder resolution approving the transaction that is being undertaken, such as a loan, purchase or rental of property.

THE IMPORTANCE OF PROTECTING YOUR CORPORATE STATUS

A corporation is a legal entity that is created and regulated by state laws. For legal, practical and tax purposes, a corporation is legally separate from any of the people who own, control, manage or operate it. If you want the advantages of having a corporation, you must follow legal requirements for running it. If you don't abide by the rules, you could find your business stripped of its corporate status—and the benefits of that status, such as:

- *Limited liability.* Corporate directors, officers and shareholders usually are not personally liable for the debts of the corporation. This means that if the corporation cannot pay its debts or other financial obligations, creditors cannot usually seize or sell a corporate investor's home, car or other personal assets.

- *Business taxes and flexibility.* A corporation is a separate taxable entity. Business income can be sheltered in the corporation among the owner-employees as they see fit to reduce their overall tax liability.

- *Employee fringe benefits.* Owner-employees of a corporation are eligible for deductible fringe benefits, such as sick pay, group term-life insurance, accident and health insurance, reimbursement of medical expenses and disability insurance.

- *Commercial loans and capital investment.* Lending institutions often give the risk-conscious corporate lender special preferences. Corporations can decide to raise substantial amounts of capital by making a public offering of their shares.

- *Business credibility.* Corporations have an air of reputability about them. In other words, although placing an "Inc." after your name will not directly increase sales, it forces you to pay serious attention to the structure and organization of your business, something that is likely to improve all aspects of your business.

- *Perpetual existence.* A corporation has an independent legal existence which continues despite changeovers in management or ownership. Of course, like any business, a corporation can be terminated by the mutual consent of the owners.

How to Use This Book

Let's face it—you've got more important and interesting work to do than spending your days reading a book about corporate forms and formalities. So, while we encourage you to read as much of this book as possible and glean as much information as you can about corporate rules and procedures, we also recognize that you may not be able or willing to spend a lot of time curled up with this material. So here are some suggestions on how to most efficiently use this book:

- Begin by reading Chapters 1 and 2. This will give you the background legal information on corporations and corporate decision-making, comparing and contrasting different ways to get things done in the corporate context. With this information, you can decide whether to (1) hold a meeting of your directors or shareholders, (2) prepare minutes for a meeting that doesn't actually occur (called a "paper" meeting), or (3) obtain the written consent of your directors or shareholders to the action or decision at hand.

- If you decide to hold a real meeting of your directors or shareholders, follow the steps covered in Chapters 3 and 4 to prepare for and hold the meeting. Then prepare the appropriate minute form to document the decisions taken at the meeting, following the step-by-step instructions in Chapter 5 or 6.

- If you opt for a "paper" meeting—one that occurs on paper only but does reflect the real decision of your board or shareholders—follow the instructions and sample forms in Chapter 7.

- If you decide to document your decision by preparing written consent forms that will be signed by the corporation's directors or shareholders, follow the instructions in Chapter 8.

If you want help writing the language to approve decisions made by your directors or shareholders at meetings or by written consent, see *Taking Care of Your Corporation, Vol. 2: Key Corporate Decisions Made Easy*, by Anthony Mancuso (Nolo Press). Chapter 9, Section C, contains a discussion of the book.

Sample forms and line-by-line instructions are provided throughout each chapter. The forms themselves are provided in two formats. Appendix C at the back of the book contains tear-out versions of all forms that you can fill in with a typewriter or pen. The corporate records disk contains text and word processor versions of each form for use on your computer. (For specific instructions on selecting and using the computer forms, see the Computer User's Guide contained in Chapter 10 of this book.)

All of this may sound like a lot. Don't worry—all of the steps and forms are covered in sequence, and we carefully explain each in detail. As you'll quickly see, there are often several approaches to accomplishing necessary tasks, meaning you can often skip good-sized chunks of material.

ABOUT THE CORPORATE RECORDS DISK

A 3½" PC/MS DOS computer disk is included in the envelope attached to the inside back cover of this book. This disk contains files for all the forms included as samples in this book. These files are provided in standard file formats that can be read into, completed and printed with your PC wordprocessing program.

Before using this disk, please read the specific instructions contained in Chapter 10, then read the **README.TXT** file included on the disk. Insert the disk in your A: drive and enter **TYPE A:README.TXT** or **MORE <A:README.TXT** at the DOS prompt to view this text file on the screen.

When to Consult a Professional

Holding corporate meetings and preparing standard corporate paperwork are usually routine tasks for smaller, privately-held corporations. But it is also a fact of business life that a particular corporate tax or corporate formality may present important legal, tax or financial considerations.

Even professionals feel the need to consult other professionals in areas that are new to them; you should avail yourself of this common sense business precaution as well. If the decision you are facing is complex, you anticipate any complications or objections, or you simply have questions and need more information, please see a tax or legal specialist before using the forms in this book. A consultation of this sort will be far more cost-effective than making the wrong decision and having to fix it later. Besides, the fees you incur should be relatively low, since you're not handing all the paperwork to the lawyer or tax person to do for you. For information on choosing and using a legal or tax professional to help you with ongoing corporate decisions and documentation, see Chapter 9.

NOTES AND ICONS

Throughout the text, we have included special notations and icons to help organize the material and underscore particular points:

 A legal or common sense tip helps you understand or comply with legal requirements.

 "Fast track" lets you know that you may be able to skip some material that doesn't apply to your situation.

 A caution to slow down and consider potential problems.

 A reminder.

 Instructions or notes about using the files on the corporate records disk.

 A suggestion to consult another book or resource.

CHAPTER 1

Corporate Documents and Laws

Calling, providing notice for, holding and voting at meetings of your directors and shareholders necessarily means becoming familiar with a bucket-full of new terminology and procedures. While mastering this material isn't difficult, it does require attention to some unfamiliar detail. In this chapter we provide legal and practical background information about basic corporate documents and the state corporation laws on which they are based.

When to Skip this Material

If you recently incorporated, are well-organized and feel you understand the purpose of your Articles, Bylaws and minutes, much of the material in this chapter may seem old-hat. If so, you may wish to skip ahead to Chapter 2, where we present an overview of the common methods of corporate decision-making, including corporate meetings and written consents.

A. Organize Your Corporate Records

Anyone who sets up a corporation needs to be able to quickly locate key organizational documents. Because these are really the constitution of your corporation, you'll refer to them again and again. When using this book to produce corporate minute and consent forms, we will often refer you to these documents.

If you have not already done so, the best approach is to set up a corporate records book that contains the key documents. You can do this on your own with a three-ring binder, or by using a customized corporate kit designed for the purpose. (You may order a corporate kit through Nolo Press; see the order page at the back of this book.)

Your corporate records book should contain:

- Articles of Incorporation (see Section A1, below)

- Bylaws (see Section A2, below)

- Minutes of the first directors meeting (see Section A3, below)

- Stock certificate stubs or a stock transfer ledger showing the names and addresses of your shareholders, as well as the number and types of shares owned by each (see Section A4, below), and

- Annual and special minutes of directors or shareholders, if any (see Section A5, below).

If someone helped you incorporate, such as a lawyer, accountant, paralegal or financial planner, you probably received copies of these documents in a corporate records book, commonly called a "corporate kit." However, some lawyers attempt to hold onto corporate records in the hope that you will have them take care of all ongoing technicalities. If so, you will need to request a copy of all corporate documents in your client file. (This is your property, so don't take "No" for an answer.)

If you can't locate a copy of your Articles, write your Secretary of State's corporate filing office and request a certified or file-stamped copy of your Articles (Appendix A lists state corporate filing offices with addresses and phone numbers). It's a good idea to call first so you can include the correct fee, which should be just a few dollars or so.

1. Articles of Incorporation

The first key organizing document all small business corporations must have is the Articles of Incorporation.[1] A corporation comes into existence when its Articles of Incorporation are filed with the state corporate filing office. The Articles normally contain fundamental structural information, such as the name of the corporation, names and addresses of its directors, its registered agent and his or her office address, and the corporation's capital stock structure.

For the majority of small corporations, there is no other important information in this document. However, larger corporations sometimes adopt Articles containing special provisions that impact future decision-making processes of the corporation.

Example: The Equity Investors Capital Corporation adopts Articles that contain a multi-class stock structure consisting of Class A Voting shares and Class B Nonvoting shares. A special article requires a vote of two-thirds of each class of stock for the approval of amendments (future changes) to the corporation's Articles or Bylaws.

To Prepare and File Articles for a New Corporation

If you have not yet formed your corporation, Nolo Press publishes several state-specific books and software that show you how to prepare and file Articles with the state's corporate filing office, and take other incorporation steps such as issuing stock under state securities laws. If you want to incorporate in California, Florida, New York or Texas, see the *How to Form Your Own Corporation* series in the Nolo catalog at the back of this book. If you want information on preparing and filing Articles only, your state's corporate filing office may provide samples and instructions for drafting your own Articles. Except in South Carolina, you do not need to involve an attorney. (Appendix A lists the names and addresses of the corporate filing office in your state.)

---

[1] In some states, the Articles go by a different name, such as the Corporate Charter or Certificate of Incorporation.

2. Bylaws

The Bylaws of a corporation are its second most important document. You do not file Bylaws with the state—they are an internal document that contains rules for holding corporate meetings and other formalities according to state corporate laws.

Bylaws typically specify the frequency of regular meetings of directors and shareholders and the call, notice, quorum and voting rules for each type of meeting. They usually contain the rules for setting up and delegating authority to special committees of the board, the rights of directors and shareholders to inspect the corporate records and books, rights of directors and officers to insurance coverage or indemnification (reimbursement by the corporation for legal fees and judgments) in the event of lawsuits, plus a number of other standard legal provisions.

Use Bylaws Over Articles for Common or Changeable Rules

State law often gives corporations a choice as to whether to place corporate operating rules and procedures in the Articles of Incorporation or Bylaws. If you have a choice, it's always best to use the Bylaws, because you can change them easily without the need for filing changes with the state. For example, many states allow you to place super-majority quorum or voting rules for directors or shareholders meetings in either document. If you use the Bylaws for this purpose, since less stringent vote requirements normally apply to the amendment of Bylaws, you can much more easily change these provisions. In contrast, if you change provisions in your Articles later, a formal amendment to the Articles must be filed with your state's corporate filing office.

Because the corporation laws of all states are subject to change, it's possible that Bylaws that were valid when adopted will later go out of date. Fortunately, major changes to corporate laws happen only every decade or two, when states modernize their corporate statutes. Nonetheless, if your corporation has been in existence for a few years and you plan a major corporate decision, such as the issuance of a new class of shares, declaration of a dividend or purchase of shares from a shareholder, it's wise to make sure your Bylaw provisions are up-to-date by checking your state's current business corporation act. See Section D, below, where we discuss how to look up the law yourself.

If You Haven't Prepared Bylaws

Some corporations may have been formed in a hurry, by filing Articles of Incorporation only. If so, you need to take the extra step of preparing basic Bylaws for your corporation. Again, if your corporation was formed in California, Florida, New York or Texas, you can use one of Nolo's *How to Form Your Own Corporation* titles to prepare state-specific Bylaws for your corporation. (See the Nolo catalog at the back of the book.)

For other states, a local law library should carry practice guides or other legal publications used by lawyers that contain sample Bylaws for your state. Or a local bookstore may carry a publication that includes Bylaws specifically prepared for use in your state. Be careful of Bylaws that claim to be prepared for use in all 50 states. There is no generic, 50-state corporation law and, therefore, no generic, 50-state Bylaw document that will work (unless it stays clear of specific rules governed by your state's laws—a difficult task).

3. Minutes of the First Directors Meeting

When most businesses incorporate, they prepare minutes of the first meeting of the corporation's board of directors or of the incorporators (the person or persons who signed and filed the Articles on behalf of the corporation). This meeting is usually referred to as the organizational meeting of the corporation. Minutes are simply a formal record of the proceedings of a meeting. The organizational meeting is usually held to approve standard items of business necessary for a new corporation to begin doing business.

Look through the minutes of your organizational meeting. These minutes are designed to document the essential organizational actions taken by the board or the incorporators. They typically show:

- the beginning tax elections made by the corporation—for example, the selection of the corporation's accounting period and tax year

- details of the corporation's first stock issuance

- approval of stock certificates and a corporate seal, and

- approval of other beginning business of the corporation, such as the opening of a corporate bank account.

Knowing some of this information may be essential to making informed corporate decisions later.

If You Don't Have Organizational Minutes

Some corporations, especially those created in a rush, simply didn't prepare minutes of the first meeting of the board of directors or incorporators. If you don't have these minutes, don't worry about it. You'll normally do fine without them.

4. Records Showing Stock Was Issued

A new corporation almost always issues stock to record the ownership interests of the persons who invest in the corporation. Most smaller corporations issue stock for cash, property or the performance of services that were rendered in forming the corporation. Many states prohibit the issuance of shares in return for a promise to pay for the shares later (in return for a promissory note) or for a promise to perform future services. If a small existing business is being incorporated, the business owners are normally issued shares in return for the transfer of business assets to the new corporation.

Example: Just Friends, a partnership, incorporates as Just Friends, Inc. Each of the three prior business owners owned an equal one-third interest in the partnership. After the transfer of the partnership assets to the corporation, each owner is issued one-third of the shares issued by the corporation (3,000 shares are issued, so each owner receives 1,000 shares in the new corporation).

If you haven't issued stock or didn't keep written records showing who owns shares, you should do so. Stock certificates and stock transfer ledgers are available in most office supply stores or can be purchased through Nolo Press. (See the corporate kit order form at the back of this book.)

Once you've organized your corporate records book, remember that while a corporate records book makes it easy for you to keep all key documents in one place, it won't work unless you consistently use it.

5. Minutes of Meetings and Written Consents

If your corporation has been in existence for some time, you may have records of annual and perhaps special corporate meetings. This is especially likely if a lawyer helped you incorporate. Check your corporate records or contact your attorney if you don't have copies. Again, remember that you have a right to these records.

B. State Corporate Filing Offices

Each state has a corporate filing office where you pay a fee and file paperwork for creating corporations, changing the corporate structure and dissolving corporations.

A listing of the name, address and telephone number of the office in each state where corporate documents are filed is provided in Appendix A. The 50 different states use slightly different names for the office where corporate filings are made; it doesn't matter what name the office goes by. Most commonly, corporations are formed with and supervised by the Secretary of State or Department of State office. The department within this bureaucracy that handles corporate filings is commonly designated as the Corporations Division or Department.

Example: Corporate filings in Illinois are made with the Corporations Division of the Secretary of State. In Pennsylvania, corporate filings are made with the Corporation Bureau, which is part of the Department of State's office. And in California, corporate documents are filed with the Corporate Division of the Secretary of State's office.

Corporation filing offices are sometimes further divided into offices that oversee special areas of concern, such as corporate filings (for example, Articles of Incorporation or Amendments to Articles), corporate name availability, corporate fee information and corporate legal counsel. Don't be put off by this seeming structural complexity. If you need information, you'll normally find there is one phone number at the corporate filing office devoted to handling corporate inquiries from the public.

Throughout this book, we refer to the office that accepts corporate filings as the state corporate filing office, whether this office is formally designated as the Secretary of State office or by some other title.

C. State Business Corporation Laws

In addition to the rules and procedures set out in corporate Articles and Bylaws, the organization and operation of a corporation are tightly regulated by a good-sized pile of laws adopted by each state. The primary source of laws that apply to your corporation will be found in your state's corporation laws (statutes), usually titled the "Business Corporation Act" (BCA) or designated with a similar name. Legal citations to sections of a state's Business Corporation Law are usually listed in the following form: "Sec. 21.2 of the Business Corporation Act" or "Article 2-12, BCA." Appendix B lists the names of all states' Business Corporation Acts.

D. Looking Up the Law Yourself

The fact is that some readers may be reluctant to venture into what they see as the musty or mysterious realm of corporate law research. To be sure, legal research of any type may seem daunting or dry, and corporate statutes are not always models of clear, concise (let alone friendly) language. Nonetheless, be reassured: looking up corporate rules is not akin to doing your own appendectomy. Corporate statutes are organized by subject matter and are well indexed and cross-referenced. For the most part, the statutes themselves state a fairly simple rule or requirement that, despite the inevitable lawyer jargon, can be comprehended by the average reader.

Most small business people can't afford to pay a lawyer upwards of $200 per hour every time they want access to basic legal information or help handling ongoing legal formalities and procedures. That's why we explain the importance of locating an experienced small business lawyer who is willing to act more like a legal coach, rather than a legal representative. (See Chapter 9, Section A.) For now, it's important to know that you can often look up the law yourself, without having to consult, and pay handsomely for, outside legal assistance.

1. Locate State Corporation Statutes

Many routine state legal rules, such as those for holding and voting at meetings, obtaining director or shareholder written consent to action without a meeting, and conducting ongoing corporate business are restated in your Articles of Incorporation and Bylaws. Nevertheless, there may be times when you will want more detail on your state's corporation statutes.

First, you need to get your hands on a copy of your state's corporate statutes. Once the statutes are in front of you, it usually only takes a minute or two to locate a relevant corporate law requirement or procedure, or to satisfy yourself that one does not exist.

Here are two easy ways to find your state's laws:

- Many state corporate filing offices provide a copy of the state's Business Corporation Act for free or for a small charge, or can refer you to a commercial publisher that sells a volume containing your state's corporate statutes. (See Appendix A for a listing of state corporate filing offices.)

- Another approach is to look up the name and legal citation for your state's Business Corporation Act in Appendix B, then go to a local law library, a law school library that is open to the public, or a larger public library with a good business collection. Ask the research librarian to show you where this material is shelved. (Most Business Corporation Acts are separately bound in one or two volumes.)

The majority of state corporation law volumes are published as annotated codes. These include annotations (references) to court cases that have relied upon, interpreted, distinguished or otherwise quoted sections of the corporation law, as well as cross-references to related code sections, law review articles and other sources of legal information on each subject matter. An annotated code helps you keep current on legal developments related to provisions found in the corporations code of your state.

THE MODEL BUSINESS CORPORATION ACT

The basic corporate statutes of many states contain the same, or quite similar, rules for organizing and operating business corporations. The reason for this uniformity is that a number of states have adopted some, most or all of the provisions of a standard law: the Model Business Corporation Act. The Act undergoes periodic changes and states are free to enact it in modified form.

The following states have enacted most, or a substantial portion, of the provisions of the Revised Model Business Corporation Act:

Arkansas	Mississippi	Tennessee
Florida	Montana	Virginia
Georgia	North Carolina	Washington
Indiana	Oregon	Wisconsin
Iowa	South Carolina	Wyoming
Kentucky		

2. Look Up Relevant Corporate Statutes

If you are not quite sure of the proper index heading to start with, browse through the table of contents at the beginning of your state's corporation act or the mini-table of contents often located at the beginning of each section heading in the act. Each heading covers major areas of corporate operation or procedure (for example, *Corporate Formation*, *Meetings*, *Stock Issuance*, *Corporate Officers*, *Records and Reports* and the like). Major headings are further broken down into sub-headings and sections that treat specific matters such as *Articles of Incorporation*, *Bylaws* and *Director and Shareholder Meetings*.

Once you are reasonably sure of the headings likely to be relevant, look up the subject matter you wish to research in the index to the corporation act at the back of the last volume of your state's corporation act. The index will eventually refer you to specific sections of the act. But as the example below illustrates, sometimes you have to patiently navigate a fairly circuitous path.

Example: To find the statute dealing with quorum requirements for directors meetings, you turn to the main entry for MEETINGS in the index. When you get these, you see that a sub-entry "Directors" refers you to "see DIRECTORS."

Under this main heading, you find a sub-entry for Meetings, with its own sub-entry for Quorum requirements. This final sub-entry, in turn, refers you to the separate Quorum sub-entry under DIRECTORS where you find the reference to the code section that specifies the number of directors required for a quorum at a directors meeting. The sample below shows excerpts from a corporations code index that reflect the results of this search—the boldface items are ones we are interested in.

EXCERPTS FROM CORPORATIONS CODE INDEX

The bold items starting at the top lead us to Corp Code Section 307 that deals with the number of members of the board required for a quorum at a directors meeting.

CORPORATIONS CODE AND RULES INDEX

. . . .

MEETINGS

    Cooperative corporations (See COOPERATIVE CORPORATIONS)

    Directors (See **DIRECTORS**)

    Fish marketing associations (See FISH MARKETING ASSOCIATIONS)

    Limited partnerships...Corp 15637

    Mutual benefit corporations (See MUTUAL BENEFIT CORPORATIONS)

MEMBERS

    Associations and clubs (See ASSOCIATIONS AND CLUBS)

    Cooperative corporations (See COOPERATIVE CORPORATIONS)

    Eleemosynary corporations...Corp 10200, 10201, 10203

(continued)

Once you use your corporate statutes a time or two, key index headings will become familiar, and you'll get the hang of moving from one to another heading. For example, to find any requirement relating to shareholders meetings, you will learn to start your search under the main heading for SHAREHOLDERS in the index, then jump down to the Meetings sub-entry under this heading.

3. Checking Other Laws

In addition to a state's Business Corporation Act, other state laws regulate special areas of corporate activity. These include:

Securities Act or Blue Sky Law.[2] These laws contain each state's rules and procedures for offering, issuing, selling and transferring shares of corporate stock and other securities.

Tax or Revenue Code. If a state imposes a corporate income or franchise tax, the state's Tax or Revenue Code will typically contain these provisions.

Commercial Code. The state's Commercial Code contains the rules for entering into and enforcing commercial contracts, promissory notes and other standard commercial documents.

Other state and local laws. Various state laws may impact the activities and operations of all businesses, whether or not they are incorporated. For example, state and local building codes, professional and occupation licensing and other laws and regulations may apply to your business and its operations.

---

[2]The term "blue sky law" was derived from the sometimes underhanded (and often colorful) practices of corporate con-artists who, in return for a small investment in their latest get-rich-quick undertaking, would promise the "blue sky" to unsuspecting investors. The securities laws of each state attempt, through stock offering qualification and disclosure requirements, to tone down the picture painted by stock promoters to a more realistic hue.

When to Use Corporate Meetings, Minutes and Written Consents

In this chapter, we provide background information on the primary ways corporations make and formally document important decisions. These methods include holding real or "paper" meetings of directors or shareholders that are documented by formal minutes, and having directors or shareholders prepare and sign written paperwork (called "consents") without the need to convene a formal meeting.

This chapter does not cover the detailed legal rules that affect these procedures; Chapters 3-8 do that. Instead, here we answer common questions about the use and usefulness of each of these procedures. After you go through this material, you should be able to comfortably decide when to hold formal corporate meetings or document corporate decisions without a meeting.

Check Your Bylaws for the Legal Rules

The legal rules and procedures for holding formal meetings or obtaining the written consents of your directors or shareholders in lieu of a meeting should be stated in your Bylaws. (If you can't locate your Bylaws, or you're not sure they are current, follow the suggestions in Chapter 1, Section D.)

A. Three Ways to Make and Document Formal Corporate Decisions

There are three basic ways to make and document formal corporate decisions made by a corporation's board of directors or shareholders. They are:

- real meeting with minutes
- "paper" meeting with minutes, and
- action by written consent.

Legally, it makes no difference which way—or ways—you settle on.

1. Real Meeting With Minutes

Your directors or shareholders and all interested parties get together in a real meeting and discuss and vote on items of corporate business. During or after the meeting, written minutes are prepared showing the date, time, place and purpose of the meeting and the decisions (resolutions) approved by the board of directors or shareholders.

2. Paper Meeting With Minutes

Under this procedure, the directors or shareholders informally agree to a specific corporate action or actions, such as the election of new directors. Then minutes are prepared as though the decision were approved at a real meeting of directors or shareholders. We call meetings of this sort "paper" meetings, since the meeting takes place on paper only.

A paper meeting is often used by corporations that do not want to go to the trouble of holding a real meeting, but do want to maintain a corporate records history, complete with traditional formal minutes. While not specifically sanctioned under corporate statutes, a paper meeting with minutes is a common form of corporate documentation. It should present no problems as long as the decisions reflected in the minutes of the paper meeting represent actual decisions reached by your board or shareholders. This procedure is quite similar to taking action by written consent, discussed below, with one key difference: formal minutes are prepared when a paper meeting is held.

3. Action by Written Consent

This is the quickest and least formal way of taking formal corporate action. The directors or shareholders consent to a decision or action in writing by signing a written consent form. Minutes for a real or "paper" meeting are not prepared. Only the written consent forms are kept in the corporate records book, to indicate that directors and shareholders made necessary decisions.

B. Questions and Answers About Corporate Meetings, Minutes and Written Consents

How to Proceed If You Are Ready to Act

If you are already sure of how you want to conduct your official corporate business, you may want to skip the rest of this chapter. Here is where to go next:

- *Real meeting with minutes.* Chapters 3 and 4 cover the steps necessary to hold a real meeting of directors and shareholders. Then Chapters 5 and 6 show how to prepare minutes to document the decisions reached at those meetings.
- *Paper meeting with minutes.* Chapter 7 explains how to prepare written minutes for a paper meeting to document a decision as though it were reached at a real meeting.
- *Action by written consent.* Chapter 8 covers the procedure and forms necessary to obtain director and shareholder approval by written consent.

The questions and answers below shed light on the advantages and disadvantages of each of the three corporate decision-making formalities. It's important to recognize that there is no one best way for all corporations to proceed. Corporations, large and small, take advantage of each of the foregoing procedures to varying degrees, depending on the nature of their business, the type of decision involved and the amount of time available to make and document a particular decision. Your best tack is to read this material thoroughly and then consider which approach is best for you.

1. How Should You Choose a Method for Documenting Corporate Decisions?

Each of the three ways of reaching and documenting formal corporate decisions has its own advantages. You'll simply need to settle on the approach—or approaches—that best suits your corporation's needs and temperament.

A real meeting allows the participants to meet face-to-face and arrive at decisions that require the give-and-take of conversation, argument or persuasion engaged in by participants. A paper meeting, like a real meeting, also results in the preparation of formal minutes that document board or shareholder decisions, but does not require the time and effort involved in getting everyone together in a meeting. The written consent procedure is the quickest and simplest of all, allowing the board or shareholders to agree to an uncontested item of business with a minimum of formality and paperwork.

Sometimes it will be clear that you really do need to hold a formal meeting. In other situations, it would be a waste of time to do so. Sometimes, any one or two, or even all three, approaches will serve you well. In other words, you can utilize whichever method works best under the circumstances.

If after reading what follows you are still unsure of what to do, seek out a self-help law coach. (See Chapter 9.)

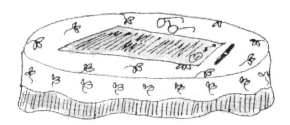

2. When Should Corporations Hold Formal Meetings?

Corporate statutes usually require annual board of directors and shareholders meetings. These meetings are usually scheduled in the corporation's Bylaws. The annual shareholders meeting is held first, in order to elect the board for the upcoming year. After the shareholders meeting, and usually on the same day, the annual directors meeting is held. At this meeting, the directors accept their positions for the upcoming year and tend to any business and corporate planning that is appropriate.

All other meetings of the board or shareholders are special meetings, which may be called any time during the year according to rules contained in the Bylaws. Special meetings may be called to discuss urgent items of business or approve legal or tax formalities that arise from time to time. For example, a special meeting might be called to approve the adoption of a new corporate tax year recommended by the corporation's accountant, to approve the conditions of a corporate loan made to an officer of the corporation or to approve a bank loan or real estate transaction.

3. Why Bother to Document Corporate Decisions?

Corporate minutes and consent forms serve a dual role: they not only show that important corporate decisions were reached with the proper notice and vote of your directors or shareholders, they also allow you to set out the reasons for these decisions. This can be crucial later if a corporate decision is examined by the IRS as part of a tax audit or scrutinized by a court as evidence in a lawsuit. In other words: One of the main reasons for preparing minutes is to document and substantiate important corporate decisions.

Likewise, your minutes may be used to document corporate strategies and decisions to incur expenses that might later be the subject of controversy or even lawsuits. Examples include the settling of a claim against a disgruntled employee or shareholder or the decision to implement safeguards in a hazardous location or line of corporate activity (for example, paying for protective measures for pedestrians at a construction site or implementing manufacturing controls in producing a consumer product).

Another simple reason to prepare regular minutes, even if your directors don't need to meet to reach a decision, is that it looks good. If, for example, you later sell your business, a formal recordkeeping system can serve you well. Also, minutes can be important, in and of themselves, to show that you are respecting, and are entitled to the benefits that arise from, the separate legal and tax status of your corporation.

Example: The IRS audits your closely-held corporation and requests copies of minutes of all annual and special meetings of your corporation. If your corporate record book is bare, or contains minutes for just a few meetings over the life of your corporation, the IRS will be less inclined to see your side of any tax disputes that may arise during the course of the audit (such as the reasonableness of salaries or bonuses paid to the shareholder-employees of your small corporation).

Also realize that you risk losing the benefit of a corporate structure if you don't comply with paperwork required of corporations. For instance, a court may decide to disregard the corporate entity and hold the shareholders personally liable for claims against the corporation if people running the business have not undertaken standard corporate formalities and procedures, such as holding and documenting meetings, issuing stock and keeping corporate funds separate from personal funds.

4. What Paperwork Should a Corporation Prepare?

Here's our recommendation for your paper trail. At a minimum, prepare written minutes (either for real or paper meetings) for all annual meetings scheduled in your Bylaws. Typically, this means preparing minutes for an annual shareholders meeting followed by minutes for an annual directors meeting.

Also prepare formal corporate documentation for all important legal, tax, financial or business decisions reached by the directors or shareholders during the year. This documentation can be in the form of minutes for a special meeting—again, either real or on paper—or written consent forms signed by your directors or shareholders.

By preparing this simple paperwork, you will have prepared a paper trail of important corporate decisions, which should give your corporate records book enough girth to help satisfy courts, the IRS and others that you attended to the necessary legal and tax niceties.

5. When Can Written Consents Be Used Safely?

Legally, written consents work just as well as written minutes of meetings to document director or shareholder decisions. They are, moreover, the quickest way to approve and document a formal decision by the corporation's board or shareholders, since they do not require time and effort to hold a meeting (or document a paper meeting) and prepare minutes. Directors or shareholders simply sign a consent form that states the action or business approved. The written consent form is then placed in the corporate records book as proof of the decision.

But written consents do have weaknesses. Depending on the situation, you may decide to use written consents anyway, but you should do so after careful consideration of the problems. Okay, so what's the downside?

If a number of directors or shareholders are involved (especially when some do not directly work in the business), a request to sign a written consent form may come as a surprise to an outside director or shareholder. As explained in Section B7, below, many corporations decide that a real meeting works best to let outsiders in on the reasons for important corporate decisions.

The IRS and the courts usually expect to see written minutes, at least for basic corporate formalities such as the annual directors and shareholders meetings. Most corporations decide that written minutes look better, and are more appropriate, to document the proceedings of annual directors and shareholders meetings, even if a real meeting is not necessary because decisions are routine and all shareholders and directors agree to the proposed decision.

All this being said, however, there is still a role for the written consent procedure in some circumstances:

- *One-person or two-people corporations.* Written consent forms are particularly useful in one-person corporations where one individual owns and manages the corporation as its only shareholder and director. The consent form procedure allows the sole corporate director-shareholder to formally approve corporate decisions without going to the trouble of preparing minutes for a pretend meeting. The same holds true for corporations where two people who work closely are the only shareholders of a corporation.

- *To document noncontroversial or time-sensitive decisions.* Particularly where time is of the essence and where a face-to-face meeting of directors or shareholders is not necessary, it may make sense to take action by written consent. There shouldn't be a problem as long as minutes are kept for annual meetings and meetings where important decisions are discussed.

Example 1: Better Mousetraps, Inc. is advised by its accountant to pass a board resolution approving a change in tax year. After discussing this issue briefly, its directors ask the corporate secretary to prepare a written consent form for the directors to sign that shows their approval of the tax election. They see no need to meet in person to approve the decision or to prepare paper minutes for a fictitious meeting. Either of these procedures seems like overkill for this simple tax formality.

Example 2: The treasurer of Best Business Bureaus, Corp., a commercial furniture supplier, decides to ask directors to approve a corporate 401(k) profit sharing plan for employees. A special meeting of directors is scheduled to discuss whether the corporation would make matching contributions for employees and to hear various corporate personnel, including the chairperson of the Employee Benefits Committee, who wish to present different opinions to the board on the advisability of adopting a plan and the level of corporate contributions to be made.

At this meeting, comments and feedback are exchanged before the board reaches decisions on the options presented under the plan. This allows the directors a chance to discuss the financial implications and pros and cons of this important piece of corporate business.

6. What's the Best Way to Hold Meetings for Closely-Held Corporations?

A small, closely-held corporation has only a few shareholders and directors. In closely-held corporations, annual meetings of directors and shareholders are held mostly as a formality. At the annual shareholders meeting, the current board of directors is usually elected, en masse, to a new term (usually one year). At the annual directors meeting, each current director routinely accepts office for the upcoming year.

Unless the election, or re-election, of a director is contested or an important item of business needs to be raised at an annual shareholders or directors meeting, many small corporations dispense with holding real annual meetings. Instead, the secretary of the corporation prepares minutes for a paper meeting showing the election of the board plus any other business the shareholders and directors agree upon in advance.

Example: Windows, Drapes, Sofas and Ottomans, Inc. is a closely-held corporation owned and run by Saul and Barbara, a married couple. They prepare minutes for the corporation's annual shareholders and directors meetings, since both are required to be held annually under provisions of the Bylaws of the corporation. Of course, Saul and Barbara plan to re-elect each other to the board again this year, and they discuss and plan corporate operations all the time. So their annual meetings are held on paper only. They prepare minutes for each of these paper meetings and place them in the corporate records book.

A "CLOSELY-HELD" CORPORATION IS NOT A "CLOSE" CORPORATION

A "close" corporation is a specific type of small corporation set up in a corporation's Articles under special state corporation laws. A close corporation can dispense with a board of directors and operate under the terms of a special close corporation shareholders agreement. Most small corporations do not bother with this special type of corporate entity, since corporate shareholders as well as outside lenders prefer to deal with a regular corporation where the board of directors and shareholders have traditional roles and responsibilities under state law. This book does not apply to the operations of close corporations.

The term "closely-held" corporation has a different, less legal meaning and is used loosely in the business world. Generally, it is used to refer to a corporation owned and operated by a small number of people who work in the business and who restrict the sale of their shares to outsiders. When we use the term "closely-held" corporation, this is what we mean.

Special meetings of the board and shareholders of small corporations follow a similar pattern. If the resolution or business at hand is a tax or legal formality that everyone agrees must be made, special meetings are often held on paper, not in person, in small, closely-held corporations. But if the issue that forms the basis of the special meeting requires discussion, such as the approval of competing bids for a remodeling of corporate headquarters, then the directors often decide to get together for a real meeting. At the meeting, they discuss the pros and cons of the proposed business prior to making a decision and preparing minutes.

7. How Should Meetings Be Held for Corporations With Inactive Directors or Shareholders?

Corporations with at least one director or shareholder who doesn't work actively in the business often find it's best to hold annual and special meetings in person. Even if the business conducted is routine, this gives the outsiders a chance to ask questions before voting on the decision at hand.

Holding an annual meeting is particularly important for annual shareholders meetings. Even if the election of the board is a formality, holding an annual shareholders meeting allows outside shareholders a chance to catch up on corporate business and leave the meeting satisfied that their capital investment in the corporation is in safe, capable hands. In other words, an annual shareholders meeting can serve the same purpose as the annual report sent to shareholders in large, publicly-held corporations. It both informs and sells shareholders on past and future corporate operations—yes, even in small corporations, a little soft-pitch sales talk may be necessary.

Example: Flexible Fliers, Inc., a round-the-clock, go-anywhere charter airline, has three main shareholders who own a majority interest in the company and act as its only directors. Two outside shareholders, having put up a portion of the capital necessary to get the business off the ground, own minority interests in the corporation.

Each year, the corporation puts out the red carpet for the outside investors, inviting them to the annual shareholders meeting where the annual financial and business reports of the corporation are presented by the corporate secretary and president, followed by nominations and a vote for next year's board.

Although the three main shareholders obviously have the power to re-elect themselves each year and make other important corporate decisions, they go out of their way to include the outside shareholders in this decision-making process. Not only does this help give the outside directors a feeling that they are taken seriously, it gives the corporation a chance to showcase its operations and plans for future expansion. It would be legal for the corporation to prepare paper minutes for a fictional annual shareholders meeting and circulate this document (or a written consent form) to the investors for approval, but a real meeting seems like a friendlier way to interact with the investors and foster a long-term relationship. Besides, the corporation may need to ask for additional capital in the future.

By contrast, FFI's annual directors meeting is held on paper only—the directors have just spent half-a-day meeting with the outside shareholders at the annual shareholders meeting. No one sees a need to meet again so soon after this meeting. Instead, the secretary prepares minutes for a paper meeting that shows each director accepted office for the upcoming year, plus any other formalities or decisions the directors agree should be included in and approved with these minutes.

8. Do You Need to Hold Meetings or Prepare Minutes for All Corporate Decisions?

No. People who work at incorporated businesses hold many scheduled and impromptu (ad hoc) meetings throughout the year to discuss and resolve items of ongoing business. In a small corporation, the directors and shareholders, who also work for the corporation, are likely to be in attendance in their capacity as regular corporate employees without donning their director or shareholder hats.

Normally, you do not need to prepare corporate minutes or consents to document a garden-variety business or staff meeting. However, if what starts out as a routine matter of corporate business discussed at an informal meeting takes on important legal or tax overtones, you should record those decisions by preparing corporate minutes or consents. (See Sections B9 and B10, just below, for a list of the types of decisions customarily made at formal directors meetings and shareholders meetings.)

Example: Software Works Corp., a small software company, does not need to prepare minutes for its weekly product development meetings or for its sales meetings at which it makes important price, promotion or distribution decisions. But if important legal or tax decisions come up at the weekly staff meeting, they should be considered either at a board meeting or, if all directors are in agreement, by use of consent forms signed by the directors. The corporation should prepare formal documentation to record the proceedings.

9. What Decisions Should the Board of Directors Make?

The bulk of a corporation's formal decision-making is made by the board of directors. The board of directors should approve important legal, tax and financial matters or those affecting the overall management of the corporation. Typical director decisions reached at corporate meetings or agreed to by written consent include the following:

- setting officer and key employee salary amounts and fringe benefits

- amending corporate Articles of Incorporation or Bylaws (Article amendments must usually be ratified by shareholders)

- declaring dividends

- authorizing the issuance of additional shares of stock

- purchasing insurance

- approving real estate construction, lease, purchase or sale

- appointing key corporate officers and departmental managers, and

- approving the terms of the loan of money to or from shareholders, directors, officers and banks or other outsiders.

10. What Decisions Are Made (or Ratified) by Shareholders?

Corporate shareholders should meet annually, typically to elect the board to another term of office. If the board of directors serves for longer than one-year terms, or if the board is divided (classified) into groups, the shareholders may meet less frequently to elect the board. Or they may only elect a portion of the board at each annual shareholder meeting.

Shareholders are asked to participate in other corporate decisions less frequently than the board. These special shareholder decisions usually consist of structural changes to the corporation or decisions that affect the stock rights or values of the shareholders. Bylaws typically set forth the major corporate decisions that shareholders are required under state law to participate in, either by ratifying (approving) a previously-reached board decision, or by making a decision independent from the board. Typical shareholder decisions include the following:

- electing the board of directors

- ratifying amendments to Articles

- approving changes in the rights, privileges or preferences of shares issued by the corporation

- approving the sale of substantial corporate assets

- agreeing to dissolve the corporation.

WHAT HAPPENS IF DIRECTORS AND SHAREHOLDERS ARE THE SAME PEOPLE?

In small, closely-held corporations, the shareholders and directors are very often one and the same. Obtaining shareholders approval is really the same as obtaining directors approval, except the directors must put on their shareholder hats prior to attending a shareholder meeting or signing a shareholder consent form. In these situations, it's common to schedule the directors and shareholders meetings one after the other on the same day, or pass out both directors and shareholders written consent forms to each director-shareholder at the same time.

Preliminary Steps Before Holding a Corporate Meeting

If you're planning to hold a meeting of shareholders or directors, you'll need to handle a few pre-meeting procedures. These consist of calling and providing notice for the meeting according to the rules contained in your Bylaws and in your state's corporation statutes.

In this chapter, we explain how to take these legal steps prior to holding a meeting of your directors or shareholders. We also discuss practical measures you should take to get the most out of the meeting process. These typically include preparing an agenda, sending participants necessary background information, arranging for the presentation of reports and making arrangements to keep good minutes.

If You Know the Steps to Take

If you are experienced in holding corporate meetings or have used these materials previously, you may wish to skip the explanation of pre-meeting steps. If so, skip ahead to Section B, below, where we show you how prepare pre-meeting forms.

Other short-cuts. Skip to Chapter 7 if you're planning to hold a paper meeting. Or skip to Chapter 8 if you want to take action by written consent without holding a meeting.

A. Overview of Corporate Meetings

Before you dive into the mechanics of preparing for your corporate meetings, it's helpful to know where you're headed. Here are the typical steps involved in holding a meeting of directors or shareholders:

- Meeting is called (requested) by someone authorized under the Bylaws or state law to do so (Section B, Step 3).

- Notice of the time, place and purpose for the meeting is given to directors or shareholders, together with any written meeting materials (Section B, Steps 5 through 9).

- Meeting is held; business is discussed and approved by directors or shareholders (Chapter 4).

- Minutes of the meeting are prepared, signed and placed in the corporate records book (Chapters 5 and 6).

We discuss the legal requirements and normal formalities associated with each of these steps in this chapter and subsequent chapters. We also provide common sense compliance tips designed to allow you to meet (or exceed) any state law requirements. Finally, we make a number of practical suggestions as to how to hold a productive meeting—a goal that's easy to lose sight of if you become too focused on the legal rules.

One-Person or Family-Run Corporations

As discussed in Chapter 2 and further amplified in Chapter 7, corporations owned and operated by one person or by families normally don't need to pay particular attention to preliminary meeting steps, and can usually forego calling and providing notice for directors and shareholders meetings.

B. Steps to Hold a Meeting

In this section, we present and discuss the sequential steps normally taken to prepare for an upcoming meeting of directors or shareholders. You may wish to sidestep some of the preliminaries covered below—glance through these steps at least once, then use your own judgment in deciding what steps to take prior to convening your corporate meeting.

If You Need to Meet Right Away

If you don't have time to comply with the meeting call and notice requirements discussed in Steps 3 and 5, below, you may have other options. If yours is a corporation where all shareholders or directors agree, you can simply prepare a waiver of notice form and have it signed by each director or shareholder either before, at or after the meeting. (See Chapter 7, Section B, Step 1, for instructions on using this waiver form.) However, this less buttoned-down approach is definitely not recommended if there is dissension in the ranks of your shareholders or directors, since the dissidents may simply refuse to sign.

Step 1. Prepare a Meeting Folder

You may be surprised at the number of forms and other paperwork that even the most routine meeting can generate. We suggest you set aside a blank file folder for each upcoming meeting. Put the date and type of meeting on the tab for the folder—for example, "Annual Directors Meeting, July 1996" or "Special Shareholders Meeting, March 15, 1996"—and keep the folder handy.

As you create each document for your meeting, place it in this file folder. After you are through with the meeting and have prepared and completed all the paperwork, you can transfer the entire contents of the file folder into the minutes section of your corporate records book.

If you're using a computer to generate documents for your meetings, another way to keep your materials organized is to place all copies of computer files associated with a given meeting in one directory or folder on your hard disk. For example, a PC computer user may wish to create a directory named "96DRMTG" on the hard disk to hold all computer files generated for the annual 1996 meeting of directors. (Chapter 10 contains further instructions for working with the files included on the enclosed computer disk.)

Step 2. Prepare Meeting Summary Sheets

When you plan and carry out the many legal and practical details necessary to make your meeting as productive as possible, paperwork and procedures can mount up fast. To help you keep track of key dates and times, and when important notices are sent, we provide a Meeting Summary Sheet on the enclosed disk and in Appendix C. This form contains spaces for you to enter information summarizing what you have done and when you have done it. And if any questions are raised later, it also serves as an excellent record of meetings actually held by your corporation and as documentation that they were called, noticed and held correctly. Use your Meeting Summary Sheet both as a scheduler and reminder sheet for all corporate meetings.

You'll need a separate Meeting Summary Sheet for each meeting. Start by preparing forms for each of this year's annual (or regular) meetings, as specified in the Bylaws.

Note that we include room for you to insert general information on the basic call and notice requirements for meetings. Giving room for you to fill in this information on the form should help remind you of the important notice requirements as you plan your yearly list of meetings.

The corporate secretary (or other person who will call or provide notice for your meetings) should keep the Meeting Summary Sheet handy and refer to it often enough to keep track of upcoming meetings, making revisions and additions to the Meeting Summary Sheet as necessary. When and if a director, officer, shareholder or other authorized person calls for a special directors or shareholders meeting, the secretary should create a new Meeting Summary Sheet and fill in all relevant information for the meeting.

Meeting Summary Sheets Help If You Are Audited

Preparing Meeting Summary Sheets for your corporation each year can come in handy if you later need to show the IRS and others, at a glance, that you paid serious attention to the separate legal existence of your corporation. Summaries of this sort are often prepared by lawyers or tax advisors when the IRS asks to see the minutes of past corporate meetings during a tax audit. Preparing your own meeting summary forms in advance may save you time and money later.

Below is a sample of the Meeting Summary Sheet included on the disk. Fill it out as you follow the sample form with instructions below. The filename for this form is MEETSUM, followed by a three-letter filename extension according to the version of the file. For example, Word users should select and use the MEETSUM.DOC file. (See Chapter 10 for information on selecting and using the computer disk files.)

MEETING SUMMARY SHEET

Name of Corporation:

_____

Year: 19_____

Type of Meeting: ☐ Annual/Regular   or ☐ Special ❶
Meeting of: ☐ Directors   or ☐ Shareholders

Date: _____, 19_____   Time: _____:_____ ____.M. ❷

Place: _____ ❸

Meeting Called By: _____ ❹

Purpose:❺ _____

_____

Committee or Other Reports or Presentations: ❻ _____

Other Reminders or Notes: _____

Notice Required: ☐ Written   ☐ Verbal   ☐ Not Required ❼

Notice Must Be Given By Date: _____ ❽

Notice of Meeting Given To: ❾

Name	Type of Notice*	Location or Phone Number	Date Notice Given	Date Acknowledged Receipt

*Types of Notice: Written (mailed, hand-delivered); Verbal (in-person, telephone conversation, answering machine, voice mail); e-mail; Fax.

Special Instructions

❶ Check the type of meeting, whether it is annual (sometimes called a "regular" meeting in the Bylaws) or special. Indicate whether it is a directors or shareholders meeting.

❷ If you know the meeting date and time, fill that in. If you expect to hold a special meeting but are not sure of the exact date, make a note anyway of the possible meeting date as a reminder.

❸ Show the location of the meeting. Most meetings will be held at the principal office of the corporation.

LOCATION IF MEETING IS HELD IN CYBERSPACE

Some companies may decide to let technology help them get together by holding a meeting via a conference telephone call, a video conference hookup, or even a virtual meeting held via a conference on a local or national Bulletin Board System. (See Chapter 4, Step 5.) If you use of these alternate meeting methods, make sure to specify the location and method of holding these high-tech meetings on the Meeting Summary Sheet—for example, "a video conference among the following individuals located at the following video conference sites: (name the individuals and sites)."

❹ Normally, no one needs to call annual directors and shareholders meetings, as they're already scheduled in the Bylaws. The president may, however, direct the secretary to send out notices of the meeting. Special meetings of the board or shareholders are called by those authorized to do so under the Bylaws. Special meetings may be called by directors, president, a specified percentage of the shares of the corporation or others authorized under state law or established in the Bylaws. (See Step 3, below, for more on calling meetings.)

❺ For all meetings, set forth a brief statement of the purpose of the upcoming meeting. The purpose of an annual shareholders meeting will usually include "the election of directors of the corporation." The purpose of annual directors meetings is normally "acceptance by directors of their positions on the board, discussion of the past year's activities, planning of the upcoming year's operations and the transaction of any other proper business that may be brought before the meeting." If additional items of business are on the agenda for the meeting, state them separately as well.

❻ Indicate any financial, personal, planning or other reports you will wish to have presented at the meeting.

❼ Check the type of notice required for the meeting: whether written or verbal, and the date by which the required notice must be mailed or given to the directors or shareholders. If no notice is required—if, for example, your Bylaws dispense with notice of an upcoming annual directors meeting—check the "Not Required" box.

❽ Many Bylaws require at least ten days' prior notice for shareholders meetings, and at least five days' prior notice for directors meetings. Make sure you provide at least the required notice for meetings specified in your Bylaws. As a matter of courtesy and common sense, many corporations give shareholders and directors at least three or four weeks advance notice of all annual meetings, and as much notice as possible of special meetings. (See Step 4, below, for a discussion of notice requirements.)

Enter the date by which you need to send out or personally provide notice to the meeting participants.

❾ Once notice is actually given, fill in this portion of the form to show who received notice prior to a meeting, whether or not notice is required by your Bylaws or state law.

For each person given notice, show the date and manner in which notice was given for a meeting. Finally, if you have prepared or received other documentation of the giving or receipt of notice (see the Acknowledgment of Receipt and Certification of Mailing forms in Steps 7 and 9b, below), make a note that this material has been placed in the meeting folder or corporate records.

Reminder to Provide Notice

We suggest you provide prior written notice of all directors and shareholders meetings stating the time, place and purpose of the meeting, even if not legally required to do so. If you are going to go to the trouble of holding a meeting, it only makes sense to give all participants early and accurate notice of where and when it will occur, and why you are holding it. Our advice goes double if you plan to consider and vote on any issues for which there may be disagreement. You can almost bet that if dissident shareholders or directors believe you are trying to take action at a "secret meeting," this will encourage controversy and tension.

Step 3. Call the Meeting

To call a meeting of shareholders or directors, someone makes an internal request within the corporation that a meeting be scheduled. Under state law or your Bylaws, particular individuals may be empowered to call meetings. Typically, the Bylaws allow the president, members of the board, a specified percentage of shareholders, or others to call corporate meetings (see Step 3a, below). After the meeting is called, the secretary of the corporation provides notice of the meeting to all persons entitled to attend.

Check your Bylaws to determine who may call meetings of your corporation. If you have any questions, check your state's Business Corporation Act. (See Chapter 1, Section D.)

WHO MAY CALL ANNUAL AND REGULAR MEETINGS

Regular or annual meetings of directors or shareholders are not legally required to be called, because they are already scheduled in the Bylaws. The secretary of the corporation is normally designated to stay on top of annual meetings, but there is always a chance that he or she may forget to remind everyone that these meetings should be held. (To avoid this, the Meeting Summary Sheet should help. We discuss how to use this in more detail in Step 2, above.)

---

a. Who May Call Special Meetings

Special meetings need to be called by someone who is legally authorized to do so. Here are the rules:

- *Special meetings of directors.* Standard Bylaws require that special meetings of the board of directors be called by the president of the corporation, the director who acts as chairperson of the board or a specified number of directors. Other officers may be allowed to call special board meetings as well; check your Bylaws.

- *Special meetings of shareholders.* Typically, special meetings of shareholders must be called by a majority vote of the board of directors, a certain percentage of the voting shares of the corporation (often at least 10%), or by the president of the corporation.[1] But note that in all states except Massachusetts,[2] the corporation is allowed to authorize persons others than those specifically mentioned in the statutes to call shareholder meetings. Again, check your Bylaws to determine the particular persons authorized to call special shareholders meetings of your corporation.

---

[1]The corporate statutes of all states allow shareholders meetings to be called by the board of directors. All but a few states allow a set percentage of the shares (often 10%) to call a shareholders meeting. About half the states specifically authorize the president to call a shareholders meeting. State statutes are silent as to how a call is actually accomplished. By custom, however, it's considered proper for the president, or a representative of a group of concerned shareholders holding the requisite percentage of shares, to notify the secretary of the corporation of a meeting.

[2]Massachusetts requires shareholders meetings to be called by the board of directors, 10% of the shareholders or the president of the corporation. See Mass. Bus. Corp. Law § 34.

b. How and When to Call Corporate Meetings

The legal requirements for the manner and timing of calling a special directors or shareholders meeting are normally not specified under state law or in the Bylaws (but check your Bylaws just to be sure). Absent specific requirements, a meeting can be called verbally or in writing, and can be made to any corporate director or officer—we suggest the corporate secretary. However made, the call should allow enough time to:

- provide shareholders or directors with ample notice of the meeting—usually a minimum of five to ten business days (see Step 5, below), and

- prepare any necessary background material and other materials for the meeting.

Smaller corporations where directors and shareholders are in close contact and acting with substantial harmony can do fine with a simple verbal call. However, larger corporations, especially those with outside directors or shareholders, and all corporations making arrangements for a meeting at which a hot topic will be discussed, should make a written call of the meeting to create a record of the fact that the meeting was properly called well in advance.

Example 1: Pants de Lyon, Inc., a Miami clothing boutique, is a small, four-shareholder corporation, owned and operated by Stephanie, Claude and their spouses. Stephanie has been working hard to set up a pension plan for the directors/employees of the corporation. At long last, they are ready to put the plan into place. Stephanie, the president, asks Claude, the secretary, to arrange for a special directors meeting in two weeks to approve the pension plan. Stephanie and Claude inform their respective spouses of the meeting, and no formal notice is sent out.

Example 2: Brick-a-Bracs Corp., a closely-held home remodeling and furnishing company, is owned and run by two shareholder/director/employees, Kevin and Gale. In addition, five other people hold shares in the corporation. The Bylaws allow the chairperson of the board, president, vice president, secretary or any two directors to call a special meeting of directors or shareholders. Gale wants to change the name of their corporation. In addition, the corporation's accountant suggests that the directors approve a change in their fiscal year. Since Kevin is in complete agreement, and the directors meeting is largely a formality, Gale feels that verbal notice is sufficient—after all, she and Kevin are the only directors.

But when Gale calls the special shareholders meeting to discuss a change in the corporate name, she considers that a couple of the shareholders have not kept in close touch with Brick-a-Bracs and know nothing about the proposed corporate name change. Even though she is confident that a change of name will be approved by the inside shareholders, she decides it will be best to document every detail of the special meeting process, and therefore gives Kevin a written call of notice.

Example 3: Grand Plans, Inc. is a medium-size building contractor with five directors and seven shareholders. Two key shareholders conclude that the business needs more capital and, to get it, additional stock should be sold. Because doing this will affect the rights and interests of existing shareholders, the president prepares a written call of notice for a special shareholders meeting where an amendment to increase the capital stock of the corporation will be presented to the shareholders for approval. The president gives a written notice of call form to the corporate secretary six weeks before the desired date for the meeting.

c. How to Prepare a Call of Meeting Form

A written Call of Meeting form is directed to the corporate secretary. It should specify the date, time and place of the meeting, as well as the purpose of the meeting. The secretary will need ample time to prepare and send out any notices required by either Bylaws or state law for the meeting. Typically, the secretary will need to give the directors at least five business days advance notice and shareholders a minimum of ten business days advance notice. Bylaws may require a longer notice period. (See Step 5, below.) Of course, there should always be enough time to prepare reports, presentations and suggested resolutions for the meeting.

Below is a sample of the Call of Meeting form that is included on the corporate records disk. Fill it out as you follow the sample form and instructions.

The filename for this form is CALL, followed by a three-letter filename extension according to the version of the file. For example, Word users should select and use the CALL.DOC file. (See Chapter 10 for information on selecting and using computer disk files.)

CALL OF MEETING

To:

Secretary: __[name of corporate secretary]_____

Corporation: __[name of corporation]_____

Corporation Address: _____

_____

The following person(s): ❶

Name	Title	No. Shares
_____	_____	_____
_____	_____	_____

authorized under provisions of the Bylaws of __[name of corporation]__,

hereby make(s) a call and request to hold a(n) __["special," "annual" or "regular"]__ ❷ meeting of

the __["shareholders" or "directors"]__ of the corporation for the purpose(s) of: ❸

_____

_____

_____.

The date and time of the meeting requested is: ❹

_____.

The requested location for the meeting is __[the principal office of the corporation or other

location]__, state of _____.

The secretary is requested to provide all proper notices as required by the Bylaws of the

corporation and any other necessary materials to all persons entitled to attend the meeting.

Date: ❺ _____

Signed:_____

Special Instructions

❶ List the name of each person calling the meeting. In the columns to the right of the name, show whether the person is a director, officer or shareholder of the corporation and, if a shareholder, the number of shares owned by the person.

❷ Fill in "special," "annual" or "regular." Annual or regular meetings do not have to be called; they're already scheduled in the corporate Bylaws. However, if you want to call the meeting as a way of keeping track of the meeting date, it's fine to do so.

❸ In the blanks after the words "for the purpose(s) of:" briefly state the purpose of the meeting. Here are some suggestions.

- *Annual meeting of shareholders:* "electing the directors of the corporation."

- *Annual (or regular) meeting of directors.* "review of the prior year's business, discussion of corporate operations for the upcoming year, acceptance by the directors of another term of office on the board, and the transaction of any other business that may properly come before the meeting."

- *Special meetings.* State the specific purpose for which the meeting was called, for example, "approval of a stock bonus plan for employees of the corporation."

❹ If appropriate, state the specific date or general time frame when you wish the meeting to be held, such as "January 15, 1996 at 10:00 AM," "first Monday in June" or "latter half of the month of October." If an annual meeting, specify the time and date scheduled for the meeting in the Bylaws.

❺ Date the form and have each person making the call sign below the date.

When you've completed the form, place it in the folder for the upcoming meeting or in the corporate records book.

Step 4. Prepare a Meeting Participant List

It's important that everyone who is legally entitled to be notified of an upcoming meeting receive such notice. By preparing a Meeting Participant List, you'll organize your records and make sure that no one is overlooked. In addition, many states require that shareholder lists be prepared within a few days of the date notice is first sent out for the upcoming shareholders meeting.[3] The alphabetical list should show the name and address and number of shares held by each shareholder; if the corporation has issued different classes or series of shares, the names may be listed alphabetically in separate voting groups.

The corporate records disk contains a Meeting Participant List designed to provide a listing of directors or shareholders entitled to attend corporate meetings. Prepare a separate Meeting Participant List for each meeting.

The filename for this form is MEETLIST, followed by a three-letter filename extension according to the version of the file. For example, Word users should select and use the MEETLIST.DOC file. (See Chapter 10 for information on selecting and using computer disk files.)

---

[3]But some states require the list to be prepared five, ten or (in the case of Alaska) 20 days before the scheduled date of the meeting itself. Generally, if the list isn't available for inspection, a complaining shareholder can petition a court to have the meeting postponed. This sort of squabbling usually only occurs in large corporations where shareholders need to contact and petition other shareholders, or assess the strength of the competition, prior to a shareholders meeting. Also note: if all shareholders sign a waiver of notice form for the meeting (see Chapter 7, Section B, Step 1), state law will probably dispense with the legal requirement that the list be prepared prior to the meeting (although it still may need to be made available at the meeting).

MEETING PARTICIPANT LIST

Name of Corporation:

_____

Type of Meeting: ☐ Annual/Regular   or   ☐ Special

Meeting of: ☐ Directors   or   ☐ Shareholders

Meeting Date: _____, 19_____

Meeting Participants *(list names in alphabetical order):*

Name: _____

Address: _____

_____ Telephone: _____

☐ Director

☐ Shareholder: Number and Type of Shares: _____

☐ Officer: Title _____

☐ Other (position and reason for attendance): _____

Name: _____

Address: _____

_____ Telephone: _____

☐ Director

☐ Shareholder: Number and Type of Shares: _____

☐ Officer: Title _____

☐ Other (position and reason for attendance): _____

SHAREHOLDERS LIST MUST BE AVAILABLE AT MEETINGS

In some states, the corporation is required to prepare an alphabetical list of shareholders who are entitled to vote at upcoming shareholders meetings, and to have this list available for inspection by any shareholder prior to and during the meeting.

Whether or not you are required to prepare a shareholders list, it's only common sense for your corporate secretary to keep an up-to-date list of your corporation's directors and shareholders for all corporate meetings. By doing this, you'll keep track of shareholders entitled to receive notice of and attend all meetings, while complying with any shareholders list requirements in your state. One easy way to meet this requirement is to keep a shareholder ledger in your corporate records book, listing the names and addresses of your shareholders. Then, simply bring your corporate records book to all shareholders meetings.

Special Instructions

Fill in, in alphabetical order, the names, addresses and phone numbers of:

- all directors or shareholders entitled to attend the upcoming meeting, and

- others who may attend the meeting, such as officers who will present reports at the meeting.

If you need to fill in more names than the form allows, make additional copies of the paragraphs providing information about meeting participants. (The tear-out form in Appendix C gives extra pages for additional meeting participants, which may be photocopied as needed.)

For shareholder's meetings, you will normally list all current shareholders of the corporation, unless:

- some nonvoting shares have been issued to shareholders, or

- the board has set a record date (the date by which a shareholder must own stock) for the meeting that restricts the number of shareholders who can vote at the meeting (see "Record Date to Participate in Meetings" sidebar, below).

Send Notice to All Current Shareholders

In privately-held corporations (no public trading of the corporation's stock), turnovers in corporate shares occur infrequently. Record dates (the date by which a shareholder must own stock to participate in a meeting), therefore, have little significance in determining who is entitled to notice of and vote at shareholders meetings. Further, most small corporation boards of directors do not fix a record date for shareholders meetings. Unless shares have recently been sold or transferred, the simplest way to deal with this issue is to provide notice to all shareholders listed on the corporate books on the day the first notice is mailed or personally given to a shareholder. If shares have been sold within the previous two to three months, check to see what your Bylaws or previous actions of the board of directors require. If you find nothing, include all shareholders who own stock before the meeting.

When you've completed the form, place it in the folder for the upcoming meeting or in the corporate records book.

RECORD DATE TO PARTICIPATE IN MEETINGS

Your Bylaws may set a date by which a shareholder must own shares in order to be entitled to receive notice of and vote at an upcoming shareholders meeting. This date is called a "record date."

Under state law, if the Bylaws do not set a record date, the board of directors may do so. Typically, however, state law also limits how far in advance a record date may be set to be eligible to vote at a meeting. Often, the board can't require shares to be held more than 50 days (some states say 60 or 70) before the meeting. Many states also specify that a record date cannot be less than ten days before a meeting. If a record date is not set by the Bylaws or directors, the state business corporation act may set a default record date for the meeting, typically the day the first notice of the meeting is mailed or given to a shareholder.

Watch out for multiple record dates in your Bylaws. Many Bylaws also specify a record date by which a person must own shares to receive dividends or other corporate benefits. The record date we are talking about is the one for the purpose of receiving notices of, and voting at, meetings.

Step 5. Prepare Notice of the Meeting

Your next step is to provide directors or shareholders with notice of the time, place and purpose of the meeting according to the requirements in your Bylaws. If your Bylaws do not specify your state's notice provisions, we suggest common sense compliance procedures for providing notice of all meetings that should satisfy even the most stringent state law requirements.

a. Provide Notice Even If Not Required

Before we summarize the state legal requirements for providing notice of directors and shareholders meetings, we want to make an important practical point: Even when notice of a meeting is not legally required, as is normally the case for regular annual directors and shareholders meetings, you should always provide it. Your directors and shareholders can't be expected to ferret these dates out of your corporate Bylaws. As a matter of courtesy, they should always be informed well ahead of time of the time, place and purpose of all meetings.

It's particularly important to provide notice when board members or key shareholders are likely to disagree on important corporate decisions. The last thing you want is for a board member or shareholder to try and set aside a key corporate decision based on a contention that a meeting was not properly noticed.

To exceed any state's legal notice requirements, simply follow these rules:

Rule 1. Provide *written* notice of all meetings.

Rule 2. Provide notice at least five business days prior to directors meetings—unless your Bylaws require a longer prior notice period for the upcoming meeting.

Rule 3. Provide notice at least ten business days prior to shareholders meetings (unless your Bylaws require a longer prior notice period for the upcoming meeting).

Rule 4. State the purpose of the meeting in the notice.

If you follow these suggestions, you should always be in compliance with your state's strictest statutory notice of meeting rules.

When to Skip State Law Requirements

If you follow the four rules above, as a reward for good behavior, you can skip our summaries of state law requirements. Go directly to Step 5c, below, where you'll find practical tips for preparing a Notice of Meeting form.

NOTICE REQUIREMENTS IF PRIOR MEETING WAS ADJOURNED WITH UNFINISHED BUSINESS

In the world of corporate legal jargon, the word "adjournment" has two meanings. Most commonly, "adjournment" of a meeting refers to the last stage of a meeting when the business of a meeting is concluded and the meeting is ended, with the person presiding announcing, "The meeting is adjourned." However, this term is also used if a shareholders or directors meeting is carried over to another time when unfinished business can be concluded. The second meeting, in this case, is referred to as the "adjourned meeting." Statutes that refer to notice requirements for adjourned meetings use this latter meaning and specify notice requirements for the second (the carried-over) meeting.

If a shareholders meeting is adjourned to continue business at another time, there is normally no legal requirement to send out notices of the continued meeting. However, notice of the new meeting may be required if it will be held at a much later date—most states require a new notice if the adjourned meeting will be held more than 120 days after the date of the first meeting. The time period for new notice is 30 days in Arizona, Colorado, Delaware, Kansas, Maine and Oklahoma; 45 days for California.

Typically, state law does not specify a rule for providing new notice to directors of an adjourned directors meeting. There are exceptions, however. For example, California requires that new notice for an adjourned directors meeting be given to all directors not present at the first meeting if the new meeting will be held more than 24 hours from the time of the first meeting. (Cal. Corp. Code § 307(a)(4).) Check your Bylaws to be sure of the notice rules in your state.

We suggest you use common sense and send out notice for any meeting that is carried over more than a week or so from the original meeting (unless your Bylaws set a shorter standard for providing notice of the adjourned meeting). Memories are short and schedules crowded with other commitments. Besides, providing a new notice gives any shareholders or directors who happened to miss the first meeting a chance to attend the second.

b. Legal Requirements for Notice

Let's look at state requirements for providing notice of directors and shareholders meetings. Remember: laws change and exceptions may exist. Check your Bylaws and state corporation law if you have any doubts or are planning to transact controversial business at an upcoming corporate meeting.

i. Notice of Directors Meetings

State notice requirements for directors meetings are somewhat lenient, since directors are expected to follow and participate in corporate affairs on a regular basis.

Annual or regular directors meetings. The laws of many states allow the corporation to set its own notice requirements for directors meetings in its Bylaws. In a number of states, it is common for Bylaws to altogether dispense with notice of annual meetings of the board.

Special directors meetings. Some states limit notice requirements to special meetings of directors. The notice period ranges from two to four days prior to the meeting, unless a longer or shorter notice period is stated in the Bylaws.[4]

Manner of giving and contents of director notice. Generally, state law allows notice to directors to be given orally or in writing. It must include the date, time and place of the meeting. Most state laws don't require that the purpose of the directors meeting be placed in the notice; however, we always recommend that you do so.[5]

ii. Notice of Shareholders Meetings

The state law rules for providing notice of shareholders meetings are stricter than those that apply to directors meetings.

Regular and special meetings. In all states, written notice of the date, place and time of all shareholders meetings, whether annual or special, must be given to shareholders. Typically, notice must be given no more than 60 (sometimes 50) and not less than ten (sometimes less, such as five) days before the meeting.

---

[4]If not provided in the Articles or Bylaws, ten days prior notice of all directors meetings is required in Minnesota and North Dakota.

[5]Idaho and Oklahoma require that all notices of board meetings contain a statement of the purposes of the meeting.

Shareholders legally entitled to notice. Usually, all persons holding voting shares are entitled to receive written notice of a shareholders meeting, as long as the shares were acquired at least 10-70 days before the meeting. In the great majority of small corporations, this means all shareholders are both entitled to notice of, and are allowed to vote at, shareholders meetings.

Nonvoting Shares May Be Entitled to Notice

Corporations occasionally issue nonvoting shares to investors, employees and others. Nonvoting shareholders may be required to receive notice of an upcoming shareholders meeting if the rights, preferences or restrictions associated with their shares will be affected or if certain fundamental corporate changes are proposed for approval at the meeting. For example, an amendment of the Articles of Incorporation, a merger or dissolution of the corporation, or a sale of major corporate assets that is not done in the normal course of corporate business may require notice to all shareholders, voting and nonvoting. Check your Bylaws to see if special rules of this sort apply.

Manner of giving and contents of notice. All shareholder notices should be in writing. The notice should state the time, place and date of the upcoming meeting. The purpose of the meeting should also be placed in the notice. Under state law, any action generally can be taken at annual shareholder meetings, whether or not the action was listed in the notice of the annual meeting.[6] For special shareholders meetings, however, state law generally provides that only the matters listed in the notice for the meeting can be approved by the shareholders at the meeting.

Example: Time Line, Incorporated holds a special meeting of shareholders with the stated purpose of amending the Articles of the corporation to increase the shares of the corporation. But during the meeting, because the corporation anticipates issuing nonvoting shares to employees, it becomes obvious that a second class of nonvoting shares also needs to be approved. Several shareholders have strong feelings about this turn of events and refuse to address the issue in the meeting. Legally, they have the right to insistthat this new issue be dealt with in another meeting called for the specific purpose of establishing a new class of nonvoting shares, since the notice for the current meeting only mentioned increasing the existing shares. A harsh result, perhaps, but it's the law under most Bylaws.[7]

c. Fill in Notice of Meeting Form

If you have decided to provide written notice of an upcoming meeting, fill in the Notice of Meeting form included on the enclosed computer disk as you follow the sample form and instructions.

The filename for this form is NOTICE, followed by a three-letter filename extension according to the version of the file. For example, Word users should select and use the NOTICE.DOC file. (See Chapter 10 for information on selecting and using computer disk files.)

---

[6]Some states (for example, California, Massachusetts, Michigan, Nevada, New Jersey, New York and Ohio) limit the business transacted at annual meetings to matters listed in the notice of the annual meetings.

[7]Where shareholders are willing to expand the scope of the meetings, it's possible to use a shareholder consent form. These are ideal for on-the-spot-decisions that need to be approved quickly without time-consuming notices or other formalities. (See Chapter 8.)

NOTICE OF MEETING OF

_____ [name of corporation] _____

A(n) _____ ❶ meeting of the __["shareholders" or "directors"]__ of _____[name of corporation]_____ will be held at _____[location of meeting]_____, ❷ state of _____, on _____, 19___ at ___:___ __.M. ❸

The purpose(s) of the meeting is/are as follows: ❹

_____

_____

_____

❺ If you are a shareholder and cannot attend the meeting and wish to designate another person to vote your shares for you, please deliver a signed proxy form to the secretary of the corporation before the meeting. Contact the secretary if you need help obtaining or preparing this form.

_____
Signature of Secretary

Name of Secretary: _____

Corporation: _____

Address: _____

Phone: _____ Fax: _____

Special Instructions

❶ If the meeting is scheduled in your Bylaws, use the term "annual" or "regular" (some Bylaws schedule more than one meeting per year for directors or shareholders; if so, these are normally called "regular" meetings). For all other meetings, insert "special."

❷ Corporate meetings are normally held at the principal office of the corporation, although state law and corporate Bylaws usually allow director and shareholder meetings to be held anywhere within or outside the state.

❸ Make sure you schedule the meeting far enough in advance to comply with state law requirements. (See Steps 5a and 5b, above.) If you don't have time to give the required notice, then make sure to have each director or shareholder sign a written waiver of notice form as explained in Chapter 7, Section B, Step 1 (you can still prepare and send out a notice of meeting form as explained here to give your directors or shareholders advance notice, but it will not be legally effective).

❹ Succinctly state the purpose(s) of the meeting. Here are some suggestions:

- *Annual meeting of shareholders.* "electing the directors of the corporation."

- *Annual (or regular) meeting of directors.* "reviewing the prior year's business, discussing corporate operations for the upcoming year, acceptance by the directors of another term of office on the board, and the transaction of any other business that may properly come before the meeting."

- *Special meetings.* State the specific purpose for which the meeting was called, for example, "approval of a stock bonus plan for employees of the corporation."

As discussed in Step 6, below, you will probably want to send out additional background material with your notice to help your directors or shareholders understand the issues to be discussed at the upcoming meeting.

Make Sure to State the Purposes of Special Shareholders Meetings in the Written Notice Form

Under most Bylaws, you can't approve any items at a special shareholders meeting unless the general nature of the proposal was included in written notice (or waiver of notice) of the meeting. If you follow our common sense suggestions above, you've already got this requirement covered.

Use Agenda to Give Notice of All Items to Be Considered at a Meeting

One way to fully inform all potential participants of the business to be proposed at the meeting is to prepare and send out an agenda for the meeting listing all the items and business that will be discussed or proposed for approval. We discuss the preparation of an agenda further in Step 6, below. If you decide to do this, fill in this blank as follows: "see the enclosed agenda for the meeting."

❺ This is an optional paragraph that you may wish to include in a notice for an upcoming shareholders meeting. It alerts shareholders of their legal right to notify the secretary of the corporation prior to the meeting if they wish to have another person vote for them at the meeting. (For instructions on preparing a proxy form for an upcoming shareholders meeting, see Step 8, below.)

Step 6. Prepare a Pre-Meeting Information Packet

You will probably wish to include meeting materials when sending out notices of an upcoming meeting to directors and shareholders.[8]

---

[8]You may wish to provide this material even if you do not send out a formal written notice of the meeting (if you provide verbal notice of an annual shareholders meeting or dispense with notice completely by having shareholders or directors sign a written consent; see Chapter 8).

To prepare people adequately for a meeting, especially those who are not involved in the day-to-day management of the corporation, it normally makes sense to send out:

- *An agenda for the meeting.* This should include new business, as well as any unfinished business from a prior meeting.

- *Copies of reports, presentations and background material.* Include all materials that may help your directors or shareholders become informed on the issues to be decided at the upcoming meeting. Doing this not only saves time at the meeting, but helps your corporation make better decisions.

- *Copies of proposed corporate resolutions.* You can prepare your own corporate resolutions (see the instructions to any of the minute forms contained in Chapters 5 and 6). Or you can use one of the ready-made corporate resolutions contained in Nolo's *Taking Care of Your Corporation, Vol. 2: Key Corporate Decisions Made Easy,* by Anthony Mancuso.

- *Minutes of the last shareholders or directors meeting.* If you want approval of minutes from the last meeting, include a copy. To save time at the meeting, you may wish to enclose an approval form with your prior minutes to allow directors or shareholders to sign off on the last meeting's minutes before the upcoming meeting. (See Chapter 7, Section B, Step 3, for instructions on preparing an Approval of Corporate Minutes form.)

- *Shareholder proxies.* You may wish to enclose a blank proxy form with notice of a shareholders meeting if you anticipate that one or more shareholders will wish to send another person to the meeting to vote her shares. (See Step 8, below.)

- *Proof of receipt.* If you want the shareholders or directors to acknowledge that they received notice of the meeting, send an Acknowledgment of Receipt of Notice of Meeting form to be signed and returned. (See Step 7, below.)

Step 7. Prepare Acknowledgment of Receipt Forms (Optional)

For important or controversial meetings, you may wish to dot all the "i"s and cross all the "t"s by preparing documentation that helps you establish the fact that all directors or shareholders actually received notice of the meeting. This may be particularly important if you have outside directors or shareholders and don't follow our advice to provide written notice to everyone (for example, you call or provide other oral notice instead). Below are procedures and forms you can use to create a record that notice was properly received by your directors or shareholders.

Following is a sample of the Acknowledgment of Receipt of Notice of Meeting form included on the corporate records disk. Fill it in as you follow the sample form and instructions below. Note that you should fill out a separate form for each person acknowledging notice.

The filename for this form is ACKREC, followed by a three-letter filename extension according to the version of the file. For example, Word users should select and use the ACKREC.DOC file. (See Chapter 10 for information on selecting and using the computer disk files.)

ACKNOWLEDGMENT OF RECEIPT OF NOTICE OF MEETING

I received notice of a(n) __["annual," "regular" or "special"]__ meeting of the __["directors" or "shareholders"]__ of __[name of corporation]__ on __[leave date blank]__ , 19___.
The notice of meeting stated the date, time, place and purpose of the upcoming meeting.

The notice of meeting was: ❶

☐ received by fax, telephone number _____

☐ delivered orally to me in person

☐ delivered orally to me by phone call, telephone number _____

☐ left in a message on an answering machine or voice mail, telephone number

_____

☐ delivered by mail to _____

☐ delivered via e-mail, PIN number _____

☐ other: _____

Dated: _____ ❷

Signed: _____

Printed Name: _____

Please return to: ❸

Name: _____

Corporation: _____

Address: _____

Phone: _____ Fax: _____

Special Instructions

❶ Check the box to indicate how notice was received. Fill in the recipient's telephone number or other information requested.

❷ The person who received the notice should date and sign the form. You may print his or her name on the appropriate line.

❸ To ensure that you receive the acknowledgment, fill in the secretary's name, address (include city, state and zip) and fax number.

Place a copy of the acknowledgment in the folder for the upcoming meeting or in the corporate records book.

Step 8. Prepare Proxies for Shareholders Meetings (Optional)

A proxy lets a shareholder authorize another person to vote his or her shares at an upcoming shareholders meeting. Larger corporations, or those that have shareholders scattered throughout a wide geographic region, may routinely include a blank proxy form with the notice and other pre-meeting materials sent to shareholders. For smaller corporations, there is no legal requirement or practical necessity to routinely send out proxy forms. This is because most of the time there is no conflict among shareholders and no desire on the part of a shareholder who will miss a meeting to authorize someone else to vote in his or her stead.

However, in rare instances, you may be asked to provide a proxy to a shareholder prior to an upcoming meeting. The computer disk includes a proxy form that you can distribute to shareholders. It should be filled in according to the sample form and instructions provided below.

The filename for this form is PROXY, followed by a three-letter filename extension according to the version of the file. For example, Word users should select and use the PROXY.DOC file. (See Chapter 10 for information on selecting and using the computer disk files.)

PROXY

The undersigned shareholder, of _____[name of corporation]_____ authorizes

_____ ❶ to act as his/her proxy and to

represent and vote his/her shares at a(n) _["regular," or "annual" or "special"]_ meeting of

shareholders to be held at _[location of meeting]_, state of _____, on

_____, 19___ at ___:___ __.M.

Dated: _____ ❷

Signature of Shareholder: _____

Printed Name of Shareholder: _____

Please return proxy by ❸ _____, 19___ to:

Name: _____

Title: _____ ❹

Corporation: _____

Street Address: _____

City, State, Zip: _____

Fax: _____   Phone: _____

Special Instructions

❶ Leave a blank line here. The shareholder will insert the name of the proxyholder—this is the person who is authorized by the shareholder to vote his or her shares at the upcoming meeting of shareholders.

❷ Some corporate statutes limit the validity of a written proxy to as little as a six-month period, so the shareholder should date and sign the form less than six months prior to the scheduled date of the shareholder meeting.

❸ Insert the date prior to the meeting for return of the proxy to the corporate secretary. This lets the secretary know in advance that a proxyholder will attend the upcoming shareholders meeting.

❹ Normally, proxies are sent out by and returned to the corporate secretary.

Remember to place copies of all completed proxies in the folder or corporate records book for the shareholders meeting to which they apply.

Step 9. Distribute Notice Forms and Information Packet

Have the secretary of your corporation mail or personally deliver the Notice of Meeting form to your directors or shareholders, together with any pre-meeting information you prepared under Step 6, above. If the information is mailed, use the exact address of the director or shareholder as shown in your corporate records. On the Meeting Summary Sheet (Step 2, above), have the secretary complete the lines at the bottom of the form indicating how and when each director or shareholder was given the notice form. Place the notated Meeting Summary Sheet in your master folder for the meeting or your corporate records book.

A. When to Use Certified Mail

Using first class mail for notices of meetings is all that's legally required. However, if you have dissident directors or shareholders, or have another good reason to want to be able to show that a person actually received a mailed notice, send these materials by certified mail with a return receipt requested. Place the certification number or return receipt in your meeting folder or corporate records book.

OTHER WAYS TO PROVIDE NOTICE

You may occasionally decide to provide notice of corporate meetings verbally in person, by phone, answering machine or voice mail. This is particularly likely to happen in small, closely-held corporations where a few people own and run the corporation, and pay less attention to the procedural niceties of corporate life. If you give notice verbally, it's wise to prepare documentation showing how and when the verbal notice was given.

In the brave new world of the information superhighway, there are a number of electronic ways to provide and prove the giving of notice to directors and shareholders. For example, you may decide to fax or e-mail notice of an upcoming meeting instead of personally delivering or mailing written notice. Although not specifically authorized under most corporate statutes, faxing or using e-mail to send a written notice to a director or shareholder should meet the substance, if not letter, of legal notice requirements. Of course, the notice must be received by the director or shareholder within the proper number of days before the meeting.

Whatever method you use, be sure to take sensible steps to show that notice was properly sent or received by your directors or shareholders within the proper number of days before the meeting. (In Step 7, above, we explain methods of proving receipt of notice of meeting by directors and shareholders.)

a. In-House Certification of Mailing Form (Optional)

If you don't want to take the time to send notices by certified mail, you can prepare an in-house certification of mailing form. In this form, your corporate secretary certifies that notice for an upcoming meeting was properly mailed to directors or shareholders. You'll find the self-explanatory Certification of Mailing in Appendix C, and on the corporate records disk.

Make sure to attach a copy of the notice prepared and mailed by the secretary to the form, and place this paperwork in your meeting folder or corporate records book.

The filename for this form is MAILCERT, followed by a three-letter filename extension according to the version of the file. For example, Word users should select and use the MAILCERT.DOC file. (See Chapter 10 for information on selecting and using computer disk files.)

CERTIFICATION OF MAILING

I, the undersigned acting secretary of ____[name of corporation]____,
hereby certify that I caused notice of the _["regular," or "annual" or "special"]_ meeting of the
["shareholders" or "directors"] of ____[name of corporation]____, to be held on
_____, 19___, to be deposited in the United States mail, postage prepaid, on
_____, 19___, addressed to the _["shareholders" or "directors"]_ of the
corporation at their most recent addresses as shown

☐ on the books of this corporation.

☐ as follows:

A true and correct copy of such notice is attached to this certificate.

Dated: _____

Signed: _____

Printed Name: _____

CHAPTER 4

How to Hold a Meeting of Your Directors or Shareholders

In this chapter we look at the basic steps necessary to hold a successful meeting of your directors or shareholders. Don't be daunted by the fact that we present a comprehensive list of possible pre-meeting steps below. As noted, only a few of these are legally required, and you can skip and combine the others as you see fit. Also, don't worry that you'll miss an important step—the minute forms set out in the next two chapters remind you to take care of all legally required steps as you prepare those forms.

If You Know How to Hold Meetings

If you're experienced in holding meetings of directors and shareholders and wish to get right to the task of preparing your minutes, skip to Chapter 5 or 6. Likewise, if you wish to document a directors or shareholders decision without holding a real meeting, skip to Chapter 7 to prepare minutes for a paper meeting or to Chapter 8 to take action by written consent.

If You Neglect to Hold or Document a Meeting

Preparing paper minutes is a good way to document past decisions. Obviously, if you failed to hold an annual meeting last year, it's too late to hold a real meeting. This can be a problem if you undergo a tax audit or simply wish your corporate records to include past directors and shareholders meetings that were not properly documented. The best way to catch up on corporate paperwork is to follow the paper meeting approach, which allows you to quickly document decisions after the fact. (See Chapter 8.)

Step 1. Provide Call and Notice of the Meeting

Before holding your meeting, it's standard procedure to call and provide notice of the meeting according to the legal requirements contained in your

Bylaws. The steps you'll take to accomplish these tasks are fully described in Chapter 3.

To Bypass Normal Notice Requirements

If you wish to sidestep all legal requirements for calling and noticing your meeting, your directors or shareholders may sign a waiver of notice form. Dispensing with notice of an upcoming meeting is particularly appropriate for small corporations whose directors and shareholders are all involved in the business and maintain regular contact. (See Chapter 7, Section B, Step 1.)

Step 2. Prepare Agenda for the Meeting

Especially for larger meetings, the chairperson's job will be easier if he or she has a written agenda that lists the order of business for the meeting. (See Chapter 3, Section B, Step 6, for a discussion of preparing a pre-meeting agenda.) An agenda can help the chairperson keep an eye on the clock, making sure that all proposed items are covered within the time allotted for the meeting.

Step 3. Prepare Corporate Resolutions in Advance

As a practical matter, it is usually best to prepare a draft of resolutions to be introduced at a meeting ahead of time. Drafting suitable resolutions for approval at meetings involves understanding the issue involved and using language that clearly states the business or matter approved by the board of directors or shareholders.

You don't need to use fancy or legal language for your resolution; just describe as specifically as you can the transaction or matter approved by your board or shareholders in a short, concise statement. Normally, resolutions start with a preamble of the following sort: "The (board or shareholders) resolved that…" but this is not required.

Following are some examples of resolutions:

Example 1 (Bank Loan): "The board resolved that the treasurer be authorized to obtain a loan from (name of bank) for the amount of $_____ on terms he/she considers commercially reasonable."

Example 2 (Corporate Hiring): "The board approved the hiring of (name of new employee) hired in the position of (job title) at an annual salary of $_____ and in accordance with the terms of the corporation's standard employment contract."

Example 3 (Tax Year): "The board decided that the corporation shall adopt a tax year with an ending date of 3/31."

Example 4 (Amendment of Articles): "The shareholders resolved that the following new article be added to the corporation's Articles of Incorporation: (language of new article)."

Nolo's *Taking Care of Your Corporation, Vol. 2: Key Corporate Decisions Made Easy,* by Anthony Mancuso, contains ready-to-use resolutions for common corporate legal, tax, financial and business transactions. Also included in the tear-out and computer disk forms are backup forms, such as promissory notes, employment contracts and shareholder buy-sell provisions, to help you take care of the business being approved by your board or shareholders.

Step 4. Get Together to Hold the Meeting

Your next step is to have the directors or shareholders meet at the time and place specified in your notice of the meeting. Most corporate Bylaws select the principal office of the corporation as the place where meetings are held, but they usually allow meetings to be held at any location inside or outside the state as designated by the board of directors. (For a discussion of several state-of-the-art ways to hold a meeting over phone lines, computer bulletin boards or via video conference hook-ups, see Step 5, just below.)

Step 5. Hold a Meeting in Cyberspace If You Have the Equipment and Know-How

When to Skip This Material

This section is not really a separate, consecutive step in the corporate meeting process—rather, it is a discussion of alternative ways of convening corporate meetings intended to supplement the rest of this chapter. If you plan to meet in person, you can safely skip this "step" and proceed to Step 6. If you're interested in setting up a meeting without the need to get everyone together at the same physical location, we hope this step gives useful suggestions for utilizing modern technology to help streamline the corporate meeting process.

Telecommunications advances now allow a number of people to simultaneously communicate over the phone lines using telephone, video and computer conference hookups. Technological refinements should soon allow us to communicate completely unplugged using cellular and other wireless technologies to project our voices and video images over the air. In short, the fast-widening horizons of what many call "cyberspace"—that virtual meeting area of voice and image located somewhere over the phone lines, network nodes or in the atmosphere—means that corporate and business meetings can routinely be held from separate locations without the need for participants to be in the same physical location.

Most existing corporate statutes are worded broadly enough to allow directors and shareholders to meet using a means of telecommunication that allows each of the participants to hear one another simultaneously. Do the participants in a computer bulletin board conference "hear" each other, even though each person's comments are displayed on a computer screen (assuming the PCs are not equipped with sound cards that actually speak the words shown on the screen)? We think the answer is "yes" and that you should be safe in discussing and concluding business over a computer network this way. However, if you anticipate that any director or shareholder may object to a meeting that's not held in person, or if a matter to be resolved at a meeting is controversial, it's best to meet in person.

Here is a short review of three of the most common types of alternative meeting technologies available today.

Telephone conference call. Many modern office and even some home telephone systems have a built-in capability for one person to call and add additional callers in a conference call conversation. If you don't have conference call capability, the local phone company can hook up a third party to a two-person call on a one-time basis for a special charge. If you need to link additional callers, the conference center of your local phone company can arrange a multi-party telephone conference at an additional charge (on top of local and long-distance phone charges). Of course, you will have to go through a long-distance telephone carrier if you want to link up directors or shareholders in different states or in widely separated locations.

Video conference rooms. If you have substantial amounts of cash handy, you can purchase the fairly sophisticated equipment necessary to set up your own video conference facility (you'll need at least two). A less expensive, though by no means cheap, alternative is to rent the use of video conference facilities provided by a private vendor, and have your directors or shareholders assemble at the leased locations. Video conference companies have offices in most major U.S. cities, as well as many cities abroad. The cost to rent each video conference site typically starts at about $300 per hour. A more recent development involves the use of desktop video conferencing products, which allow personal computer users to set up their own video conference at significantly reduced costs. Expect the video and audio channels to be somewhat slow, with slightly delayed or staggered sounds and images, in comparison with their pricier commercial counterparts.

Computer bulletin board conference. Most large-scale national computer bulletin board systems (BBSs), such as CompuServe, Dialog or America Online, have the capacity to allow an individual user to invite others to participate in a private conference. The person coordinating the meeting notifies the other participants, each of whom must be a member of the BBS, to sign onto the board, or a particular forum on the board, at a pre-arranged time, using a password or PIN (personal identification number). As each person signs on, the meeting coordinator, who is already logged onto the board or forum, invites each participant to chat, thereby linking everyone together in one online conversation. Each participant types his or her comments on a computer screen for others to view.

To avoid confusion and fast-scrolling overlapping messages, the meeting chairperson should introduce and lead each discussion, asking each of the participants in turn for comments and votes on each matter. The secretary of the meeting can capture all dialog on the screen by saving it to a file on a computer disk. Once the meeting is concluded and each participant has signed off the board, the secretary can assemble, format and print the contents of the screen dialogue saved in the computer file, making a copy for each participant to review and approve.

FORMAL RULES FOR RUNNING A MEETING

You can plan your meeting to be as formal or informal as you wish in raising, seconding and voting on items of business. We do not include a guide to the many parliamentary rules and procedures (formal rules for conducting meetings) that can be used to run directors and shareholders meetings because we believe they are usually unnecessary. If your corporation has only a few shareholders and directors, a conversational format will probably work best. For slightly larger meetings, we have found that an agreeable, but no-nonsense, chairperson will be the main requirement to keep meetings on track.

Corporations with more than about ten directors or shareholders may need to establish more detailed ground rules for meetings. For example, you may wish to call on board members or shareholders individually to elicit comments and opinions prior to a vote, setting a time limit for remarks to five minutes or so. Or directors may wish to have motions formally proposed, seconded and discussed before the question is called and a vote taken.

If you need guidance in setting ground rules or formality, you can use formal parliamentary procedures. For a remarkably easy-to-use guide to implementing the most commonly used parliamentary procedures at meetings, see *Parliamentary Law at a Glance,* by Utter (Contemporary Books, Inc.).

Step 6. Appoint a Chairperson and Secretary

Before the meeting begins, you'll need to find people to fulfill two important roles at the meeting:

- *Chairperson.* This person, usually the president, directs the activity at the meeting.

- *Secretary.* Someone different from the chairperson acts as secretary of the meeting. He or she takes notes of the order and outcome of business discussed and voted upon at the meeting. These notes will be used later to fill in the blanks on the minutes forms as explained in succeeding chapters. In almost all cases, corporations choose the corporate secretary as the secretary for corporate meetings. In the minutes forms presented in later chapters, we assume you will follow this traditional practice.

Exactly how a meeting is organized and conducted and how each person does each job at the meeting is up to you. Aside from imposing quorum and voting requirements, state corporation law generally does not concern itself with parliamentary procedures used at meetings. For a discussion of practical steps to take to introduce, discuss and vote on proposals at corporate meetings, see Step 12, below.

Step 7. Chairperson Calls the Meeting to Order

The chairperson normally calls the meeting to order by announcing that it's time to begin. The chairperson then directs the order in which business will be covered at the meeting. Typically, the chairperson will introduce some items and call on others to take the lead for certain items of business. For example, the chairperson may ask the secretary of the meeting to read a proposal and take the votes after the issue is discussed.

NOTE-TAKING AT MEETINGS MADE EASY

The secretary of your meeting does not need to provide a longhand narrative of all the happenings at a corporate meeting. It is normally enough to list who is present, the nature of the proposals raised and the outcome of votes taken. This information can then be used to complete the minutes forms on the computer disk. The quickest method of all is for the secretary to fill in final versions of the minutes forms using a computer at the meeting and making any necessary changes on the spot.

Another workable approach is for the secretary to fill in a blank minutes form at the meeting and insert the text of resolutions as the meeting progresses. You can use the completed form as your final minutes if it is prepared neatly; or, more typically, you can use it as a draft and later transfer the information to the final version of your minutes form.

Step 8. Secretary Determines Whether a Quorum Is Present

The secretary should note those present and absent from the meeting, making sure that a quorum of directors or shares is in attendance. If you followed our suggestion in Chapter 3, Section B, Step 5, and sent written notice of the meeting to directors or shareholders ahead of time, you should have a quorum (the minimum number of directors or shareholders needed to hold a meeting). If a quorum is not present, the chairperson should adjourn the meeting to a new time and date. (See Chapter 3, Section B, Step 5, for a discussion of the requirements for providing notice for the new meeting.)

Your Bylaws should state the quorum requirements for directors and shareholders meetings. Below we discuss the typical quorum requirements found in most Bylaws.

a. Establishing a Quorum at Directors Meetings

Most Bylaws, and the laws of the various states, set a quorum for directors meetings at a majority of the authorized number of directors.[1] The authorized number of directors is the total number of slots on your board, whether or not each board position is filled.

Example: The Bylaws of XYZ Corporation state that the corporation shall have seven directors and that a majority of the authorized number of directors represents a quorum for directors meetings. Four directors, therefore, must attend board meetings for business to be discussed and approved. This is true even if any slot on the board is currently vacant.

---

[1]Some states may allow business corporations to set a higher or lower quorum in their Bylaws, as long as any lesser quorum requirement does not fall below a set statutory minimum (often established as one-third of the full board). For example, smaller corporations—often those with five or fewer members—may wish to ensure a significant director presence by imposing a two-thirds quorum requirement for board meetings.

A Quorum Must Be Present When Action Is Taken

For the directors to take action, a quorum must be present at the meeting. If a quorum of directors is not present at a directors meeting, or someone leaves and the quorum is broken, the meeting must be adjourned until another time when a quorum of directors can be obtained for the meeting.

b. Establishing a Quorum at Shareholders Meetings

Bylaws usually define a quorum for shareholders meetings as a majority of the shares (not shareholders) entitled to vote on the matters presented at the meeting.[2] For the great majority of smaller corporations that have only one class of voting shares, this means all shareholders are entitled to vote on matters presented at shareholders meetings. Note that unlike the director-meeting quorum rule, this rule relates to the number of votes, not the number of people present at a meeting. Since shareholders are given one vote per share under standard Bylaws, shareholders holding a majority of the shares must be present (in person or by proxy) to hold a shareholders meeting.

Shares represented by proxies are entitled to vote at the meeting. A proxy is a signed statement by a shareholder authorizing another person to vote his or her shares at the meeting. (See Chapter 3, Section B, Step 8, for instructions on preparing the proxy form included on the computer disk.)

If you have issued nonvoting shares or have special classes of series of shares that are excluded from voting on particular issues, you do not normally count these nonvoting shares in determining if a quorum is present.

---

[2]Some states permit this majority-quorum rule for shareholders meetings to be varied in the Articles or Bylaws. Two states, Connecticut and Ohio, provide that the shareholders present at a meeting constitute a quorum (majority of all shares not required). See Conn. Stock Corp. Act § 33-328 and Ohio Rev. Code Ann. § 1701.51. To determine your shareholder meeting quorum requirements, as always, check your Bylaws. Conversely, larger corporations with larger boards may feel encumbered with a majority-quorum rule and decide to set a board quorum at a less-than-majority percentage or number—for example, one-third the directors or eight out of 20 directors.

Example: Green Construction Corporation has 600 shares outstanding, but only 500 are voting shares. The corporation ignores the 100 nonvoting shares in its calculation of a quorum. If 300 out of the 500 voting shares attend a meeting, there is a quorum.

Voting Rules for Special Classes of Shares

In special cases—for example when asking shareholders to approve an increase in one class of stock—other classes of shares, whether voting or nonvoting, may be entitled to vote on the proposal if their interests may be adversely affected by the increase. Your Bylaws should alert you to any special situations where nonvoting shares or other special classes or series of shares may be entitled to vote at a shareholders meeting.

Unlike the rule for directors meetings, a quorum for shareholders meetings needs to be established only once, at the beginning of the meeting. Even if shareholders owning a number of shares (or individuals holding proxies) sufficient to lose a quorum leave the meeting, the remaining shareholders can continue to take valid, legal action at the meeting. The reason for allowing continued action at shareholders meetings is to counter quorum-busting tactics historically used at shareholders meetings convened by larger, publicly-traded corporations. There, persons holding significant numbers of shareholder votes would leave a meeting to prevent a shareholder vote on an item they were opposed to but didn't have sufficient votes to stop.

Be Wary When Taking Controversial Action

If you face a controversial decision in the context of a shareholders meeting where you no longer have a quorum, take heed. Some states provide that the remaining shareholders can only take action by marshaling a number of votes (shares) at least equal to a majority of the required quorum. For example, let's say 1,000 shares must be present or represented at a shareholders meeting to meet a corporation's quorum requirement. If 1,000 attend and 250 shares leave the meeting, there's no problem as long as 501 shares vote in favor of the resolution presented at the meeting. But if 500 shares or more leave, then many states prohibit any further action, since a majority of the required quorum will not be able to vote in favor of actions brought before the meeting. If your state imposes a special voting rule after the loss of a quorum at shareholders meetings, it should be restated in your Bylaws.

Step 9. Secretary Reads Minutes or Summarizes Business of Last Meeting

After determining that a quorum is present at the meeting, it is customary, but not legally required, for the secretary of the meeting to read or summarize the minutes of the last meeting, after which the minutes are approved by the participants. This is a polite and efficient way to have everyone agree that the written minutes for the prior meeting properly reflect and summarize the actions taken and decisions reached at that meeting. Often, a board member will have a small correction which can be made to the minutes. It is up to the president or chairperson to accomplish this without having meeting participants completely rehash the proceedings of the prior meeting.

Save Time by Sending Out Minutes in Advance

To save the trouble and boredom of reading and discussing minutes of a prior meeting at the current meeting, you can send them out as part of the pre-meeting packet discussed in Chapter 3, Section B, Step 6.

Step 10.   Officers and Committees Present Reports

The next item on the agenda of many meetings is for the chairperson to call on committees of the board, corporate officers, department managers and outside consultants or advisors to present or hand out presentations or reports at the meeting. Obviously, if all board members or shareholders work in the business and are fully current on its affairs, presenting formal reports may not be necessary. But when shareholders or board members are not in day-to-day contact with the business, these summaries can be extremely valuable.

Do the Dollars First

In our experience, it makes sense to review the corporation's profit and loss picture first, as these are the figures everyone is most interested in.

Reports are often made to update those present at the meeting on past or projected corporate operations or a particular aspect of corporate performance, such as the corporation's net worth reflected on the latest balance sheet or upcoming plans for increasing the corporation's market share of sales in a particular area of operation. Reports can also provide shareholders or directors with the information necessary to make an informed decision on an issue. For instance, it would be helpful to have a discussion of important options associated with the adoption of a 401(k) profit sharing plan or a report by the president explaining the reasons for the creation and issuance of a new class of shares.

Example: Prior to proposing a vote on a resolution to increase the coverage limits of the corporation's product liability insurance, the chief financial officer summarizes current coverage limits and options for increased coverage based upon data obtained from the corporation's insurance broker. Next, the corporation's outside legal advisor gives a report summarizing current trends and outcomes in product liability law cases in operations related to the corporation's product line.

One question that often arises when small corporations hold their annual shareholders meeting is whether it is better to present reports at the shareholders meeting or at the annual directors meeting that usually follows on the same day. Our preference is to present reports at the directors meeting, since this enhances the directors' protection from personal liability for decisions based on the reports. (See "The Legal and Practical Value of Reports Presented at Meetings" sidebar, below.) If you have considerably more shareholders than directors, however, it's common sense that you'll want the reports to be heard or read by as many interested people as possible and the shareholders to be kept fully informed of business operations and performance. One way to achieve these goals is to convene your shareholders meeting first to elect the directors (as you would normally). Once elections are completed, immediately adjourn the meeting and reconvene as a directors meeting, asking all nondirector-shareholders to stay to hear the reports that will be presented at this second meeting.

Example: At the annual shareholders meeting for Yolodyne Corp., the board is re-elected for another term. The shareholders meeting is adjourned, and the annual directors meeting convened with all shareholders still in attendance. At the directors meeting, the chairperson calls on the treasurer to report on past and projected balance sheet figures, followed by a report by the president outlining new operations planned for the upcoming year. Providing past and prospective information of this sort to shareholders (as well as directors) can be essential to keep outside investors satisfied with the work goals and performance of the corporate management and staff.

Try to Avoid Presenting Completely New Material

To save time at meetings, and to avoid surprise, we recommend that reports and background information be mailed to directors or shareholders prior to the meeting. (See Chapter 3, Section B, Step 6.) The presentors can then restrict their comments to reviewing the gist of the circulated report, emphasizing the most important points.

THE LEGAL AND PRACTICAL VALUE OF REPORTS PRESENTED AT MEETINGS

In an effort to give corporate board members an additional measure of legal protection—and to increase their comfort level when discharging their managerial duties—the statutes of many states specifically immunize a director from personal liability if he or she relied on these reports when reaching a decision, unless the director knew, or should have known, that the information submitted in the report was unreliable.

Reports at shareholders meetings can have another, broader purpose: they are an excellent way to keep shareholders informed of corporate operations and performance. Such reports not only provide a good jumping off point for discussion at the meeting, they can also head off objections by shareholders who otherwise might claim that they hadn't been kept informed.

Step 11. Handle Any Unfinished Business

No matter how long meetings last, at least one item of business is often carried over to the next meeting. If this happened at your last directors or shareholders meeting, make sure to tackle any old work first before taking care of the new business on the agenda. Of course, any notice (or waiver of notice) for the current meeting should have included a summary of any unfinished business to be considered at the meeting.

Step 12. Introduce and Discuss Specific Proposals

After any reports or background presentations have been made at the meeting, the chairperson or another board member will normally want to formally introduce proposals for discussion and vote by the directors or shareholders. Proposals are best introduced in the form of resolutions that clearly and legally state the item or business or matter to be approved. This allows you to include the exact language of the resolution in your minutes, with no need to reword it later.

Resolutions Reminder

Short and simple, not legal, language works best when wording your own resolutions. See the examples given in Step 3, above.

a. Procedure for Introducing Resolutions at Directors Meetings

The procedures used by corporations to introduce, discuss and decide board of directors resolutions take many forms. Typically, the chairperson or another participant at the board meeting follows a prepared agenda to introduce a proposal to be discussed, such as whether or not to increase the liability limits of the corporation's general liability insurance policy. The proposal can be introduced by way of a formal motion that is seconded by another participant and then discussed. Or a proposal can simply be introduced by the chairperson with the assumption that some discussion will occur before a formal motion is made.

Either way, a discussion of the merits and possible parameters of the proposal is likely unless all board members are already fully informed and ready to vote. For example, the president, acting as chairperson, might introduce an agenda item consisting of a resolution to increase corporate insurance coverage. The board members discuss whether and how much extra insurance coverage is necessary. Once the general discussion is over, a board member can either propose adopting the resolution if one has been introduced, or propose specific language for the proposal.

After a resolution has been introduced and discussed, or vice versa, it's normal to move for a voice vote on the resolution. However, experienced chairpersons, aware of the desirability of achieving a consensus, will be sensitive to divergent views and, if consistent with getting necessary business accomplished, will normally allow members to suggest modifications to the resolution prior to calling for a vote. For example, a member may propose a resolution asking for the purchase of $50,000 additional liability coverage by the corporation. Another board member may propose that the insurance resolution be made more specific by authorizing the purchase of $50,000 of general liability insurance coverage from the lowest bidder, after getting quotes from the corporation's current insurance carrier and outside companies.

After the language of a resolution is decided, the directors or shareholders vote to approve or disapprove it. (See Step 13, below.) If a resolution passes, it is inserted in the minutes for the meeting and becomes the official act of the corporation. If it fails, it normally isn't mentioned in the minutes, unless you want a record stating that the resolution didn't pass.

b. Procedure for Introducing Resolutions at Shareholders Meetings

The shareholders are authorized to elect the board of directors at the annual (or regular) shareholders meeting. The bulk of formal corporate decision-making is performed by the board of directors. However, from time to time, the corporation may be required under state law, or may voluntarily decide, to seek shareholder approval of major corporate actions or structural changes to the corporation. Such decisions might include the decision to amend the Articles of Incorporation, a plan of merger or dissolution, and the like. When you do seek shareholder approval of a resolution, you will want to prepare shareholders in advance and allow for a full discussion of the resolution by the shareholders prior to taking a vote. (For a discussion of the decision-making roles of directors and shareholders, see Chapter 2, Section B9, "What Decisions Should the Board of Directors Make?" and Section B10, "What Decisions Are Made (or Ratified) by Shareholders?")

The specific language of shareholders resolutions is not normally drafted and discussed at shareholders meetings. Instead, this language is usually worked out in advance by the board or officers of the corporation. Typically, the shareholders were mailed background material and any draft resolutions prior to the meeting. At the meeting, they are simply asked to ratify the language of a resolution already proposed and approved by the directors at a directors meeting. Of course, depending on the style of your shareholders meetings, reports and other background material may be presented at the meeting prior to taking a shareholder vote.

Example: At the annual shareholders meeting of the Rackafrax Corporation, the shareholders are asked to ratify an amendment to the Articles of Incorporation that increases the number of authorized shares of the corporation. The resolution presented for approval at the shareholders meeting is a copy of a resolution drafted and approved earlier by the board of directors. This resolution, together with a written summary of the reasons for the amendment, is sent out to the Rackafrax shareholders along with notice for the meeting as part of the pre-meeting materials mailed in advance to each shareholder. (See Chapter 3, Section B, Step 6.)

At the shareholders meeting, the resolution is introduced by the chairperson, then time is taken for a discussion of the resolution by the shareholders, corporate officers and staff present at the meeting. Following this discussion, the chairperson makes a motion for a shareholder vote on the written resolution. After being seconded, the motion carries and a shareholder vote on the amendment is taken. The only other important item of business raised at the Rackafrax meeting is the election of the board of directors for another term of office. The president (chairperson) moves that all existing directors be re-elected. A vote is taken and the shareholders approve the re-election of the board. The shareholders meeting is adjourned, and the board members reconvene to hold the annual directors meeting.

Step 13. Take the Votes of Directors or Shareholders

After resolutions have been presented in final form at a meeting, they must be voted upon by the board of directors or shareholders. For most resolutions, the majority vote of those present at a meeting (at which a quorum is present) must be obtained. Below, we summarize the state law voting rules for director and shareholder approval of resolutions at meetings.

a. Voting Rules at Board of Directors Meetings

In all states, unless the Articles or Bylaws specify otherwise, the board of directors may legally act by the approval of a majority of the directors present at the meeting. Bear in mind, of course, that a sufficient number of directors must be present to represent a quorum of directors.

Example: A quorum of three (of five authorized) directors attends a board meeting. The votes of two of the three directors present at the meeting are necessary to pass a resolution.

Following are some key issues that may arise during the voting process.

If a director abstains. When a director abstains, it often means he or she doesn't agree to a particular action, but simultaneously doesn't want to annoy others by voting "no." In short, a director may want to duck the issue by having the minutes reflect a neutral position. That's fine, but it is also important to understand that a director abstention is treated the same as a "no" vote for purposes of the vote needed to pass a resolution. Put another way, if five directors are present at a meeting, you need three "yes" votes to pass a resolution. With two "yes" votes, two "no" votes and an abstention, the resolution fails.

Liability of silent directors. Most states specify that a director may be held liable for decisions made at meetings if the director remains silent. In other words, if the board approves a decision that later results in liability of the board (because of a grossly negligent or unlawful action approved at a board meeting), the silent directors may be found liable for the decision as well as those who voted for the proposal. Under the typical state statute, a director present at a meeting may be charged with having said "yes" to corporate action taken at a directors meeting unless the director:

- objects to the holding of the meeting

- abstains from the vote, or

- votes "no" to a proposal.[3]

---

[3]The corporate statutes of most states contain a provision that holds silent directors to have agreed to action taken at a board meeting. Six states have laws that assume assent by silent directors only for specific types of decisions for which liability may be imposed on directors. Only seven states do not attribute assent to corporate action by a silent director: Delaware, Kansas, Louisiana, Massachusetts, Missouri, Nevada and Oklahoma.

If you have doubts about a proposal submitted at your board meeting, vote "no" or "abstain," but don't pass on the proposal or otherwise remain silent as a means of expressing your opinion.

Method of voting. Unless a specific request for a written vote (ballot) is presented at the meeting, voice votes are normally taken on resolutions brought before board meetings. By the time a vote occurs, often everyone is ready to say "yes." But this isn't always the case. If there is any opposition, it's usually best to poll the board by asking each member to voice his or her vote individually. Written ballots are normally only requested when the issue at hand is controversial or contested and members of the board don't wish to announce their decision at the meeting.

b. Voting Rules at Shareholders Meetings

Every state provides that each voting share of a corporation is entitled to one vote per share unless the Articles of Incorporation provide otherwise. Unless otherwise specified in the Articles or Bylaws, resolutions must be approved by a majority of the number of shares represented at a meeting either in person or by proxy.[4]

Example: In a corporation that has issued 10,000 voting shares, shareholders owning 8,000 shares attend a shareholder meeting. Action must be taken by the vote of at least 4,001 shares—a majority of the shares present at the meeting.[5]

---

[4]Massachusetts is the only state that does not specify a default rule of a majority of shares represented at a meeting for normal shareholder voting. Massachusetts Bylaws, like those prepared in other states, customarily provide that the vote of a majority of shares represented at a meeting at which a quorum is present is necessary for shareholder approval of a resolution.

[5]In unusual circumstances, the number of shares represented at a meeting may be less than a quorum. This is so because shareholder meetings can normally continue to convene and take action despite the loss of a quorum following the departure of shareholders from the meeting. (See Step 8, above.)

Reminder

Shareholders can sign a proxy form that allows another person to vote shares at a meeting. (See Chapter 3, Section B, Step 8, for a discussion of proxies and instructions on preparing proxy forms for shareholder voting.)

ARTICLES OR BYLAWS MAY CONTAIN SPECIAL VOTING RULES

Your Articles or Bylaws may require the vote of more than a majority of shares for the approval of special types of proposals. Typically, there must be approval by a majority or two-thirds of the outstanding shares of the corporation for such important matters as:

- the amendment of Articles of Incorporation

- the dissolution of the corporation after the issuance of shares, or

- the sale of substantially all corporate assets not in the ordinary course of business.

Very rarely, the Articles or Bylaws give one class or series of shares the right to a separate vote on certain proposals. So, if decisions fundamental to the organization or operation of your corporation are to be made, check your Articles and Bylaws for special provisions. If you find any, make sure you understand what is required and check your conclusions with your legal advisor.

A relatively small number of states—including California, Connecticut, Delaware, Kansas, Louisiana, Maine, Minnesota, New Jersey, New Mexico, North Dakota, Oklahoma and Virginia—allow the Articles to give voting rights to outsiders who hold bonds issued by the corporation. This is one method of giving control of corporate policies (by participation in board elections) to corporate creditors. Another is appointing a corporate noteholder as proxy to vote a block of shares owned by corporate shareholders. If your corporation has issued notes or bonds to outsiders, make sure you know the voting rights of these corporate bond or note holders by checking your Articles and Bylaws.

Following are some topics that may come up in the course of a shareholder vote.

How shareholder abstentions are counted. The traditional rule, still followed by a majority of the states, is that shareholders must approve a resolution at a meeting by a majority of shares present, with abstentions counted as "no" votes. The following states have adopted this rule: Alabama, Alaska, Arizona, California, Colorado, Connecticut, Delaware, District of Columbia, Hawaii, Idaho, Illinois, Kansas, Louisiana, Maine, Maryland, Michigan, Minnesota, Missouri, Nebraska, Nevada, New Hampshire, New Jersey, New Mexico, New York, North Dakota, Oklahoma, Pennsylvania, Rhode Island, South Dakota, Texas, Utah, Vermont and West Virginia.

Example: In a corporation with 100 outstanding voting shares, shareholders owning 70 voting shares attend a meeting. Shareholders with 33 shares vote in favor of a proposal, 27 shares vote against, and ten shares abstain. The proposal fails because a majority of those shares present—at least 36—did not vote in favor of the matter (all shares not affirmatively voting "yes" are treated as "no" votes). Strangely, if the ten abstaining shares had not attended the meeting, the proposal would have passed—a quorum of 60 shares would have been in attendance, with a majority of the 60 shares present (33) voting in favor of the proposal.

The way shareholder abstentions are counted has begun to change. The modern shareholder approval voting requirement, adopted in Section 7.25(c) of the Model Business Corporation Act and in the corporate statutes of a substantial minority of states, simply requires that the number of votes cast in favor of a proposal at a meeting must exceed the number cast against it, with abstaining votes not counted either way. Of course, a quorum must be present initially at the meeting in order for any proposal to be submitted to the shareholders for a vote. The redefinition of the normal majority approval rule eliminates the problem of shareholder abstentions illustrated above. This MBCA section has been adopted in Arkansas, Florida, Georgia, Indiana, Iowa, Kentucky, Mississippi, Montana, North Carolina, Oregon, South Carolina, Tennessee, Virginia, Washington, Wisconsin and Wyoming.

Example: Assume the same facts as above for a corporation with 100 voting shares. Seventy voting shares attend a meeting, 33 shares vote in favor of a proposal and 27 shares vote against it, with ten shares abstaining. The resolution would pass in a state with the modern shareholder voting rule.

Note that this modern shareholder abstention rule normally does not apply to the election of directors, where a majority of those present at a meeting must affirmatively vote in favor of nominees to elect them to the board.

Method of voting. Shareholder votes are normally taken as voice votes, with each shareholder announcing the number of shares voted for a proposal. Of course, a particular shareholder normally votes all of her shares for or against a proposal, though this is not legally required. Generally, you are free to take written ballots of votes instead of voice votes if you wish; if a shareholder requests a special polled or written vote, it is customary to allow it.

Election of directors. The main job of shareholders convened at their annual meeting is to elect directors of the corporation for the next year. Normally, this is done by taking the voice votes of shareholders, with the directors receiving the highest number of votes being elected to the board—for example, the top three vote-getters from five nominees are elected to a three-person board.

Corporate Bylaws sometimes contain specific provisions, based upon state statutes, that specify special voting procedures to be followed to nominate and elect directors. For example, some Bylaws may provide that any shareholder may request the election of directors by written ballot.

Also, the Articles or Bylaws of the corporation may require or allow cumulative voting—a special type of voting process used primarily to protect minority shareholder interests in larger corporations—for directors by the shareholders. (See "Cumulative Voting by Shareholders" sidebar, below.) And in some states, even if cumulative voting is not mentioned in the Articles or Bylaws, it may be requested by a shareholder when electing the board to another term. Although you should be aware of the existence of this special shareholder voting procedure, it rarely has relevance to small corporations with roughly proportionate share ownership, since the outcome of a cumulative and a regular (one share-one vote) election in these corporations is usually the same. Again, your Articles and Bylaws should alert you to when or whether cumulative voting must be used to elect directors in your state.

Although you need to pay attention to election procedures contained in your Bylaws, don't obsess on them—unless, of course, a board position is contested. In such cases, you will want to be extremely careful to follow the correct procedure and may even want to double-check with a legal advisor.

(See Chapter 9.) Since it's rare to have a contested director election for a small business corporation, you'll normally do just fine by following our suggestions for providing shareholders with advance written notice of all shareholders meetings, together with a list of candidates for the board. (See Chapter 3, Section B, Step 6.)

Terms of office. Corporate laws normally require the election of directors each year by the shareholders. There is, however, no limit under state law on the number of times any individual may be re-elected to serve another term on the board.

Shareholders of Small Corporations Normally Re-elect the Entire Board

Except in the case of controversy or ill-will among corporate principals, or the retirement or disability of a director,[6] small corporations routinely re-elect the corporate board to serve another term at each annual meeting of shareholders.[7]

---

[6]State law and standard Bylaws normally allow the remaining board members to elect a person to fill the unexpired term of a vacant board position.

[7]Of course, if your state allows your corporation to elect directors for terms longer than one year, then shareholders meetings for the election of the board may be held every other year (for two-year director terms) or at some other interval. Also, if your corporation has opted for a classified board (with some directors elected every so many years), then only a portion of the board will be elected every year.

CUMULATIVE VOTING BY SHAREHOLDERS

Cumulative voting by shareholders in the election of directors can help protect minority shareholder interests in larger corporations. If your Bylaws require the use of cumulative voting in an election of directors, then each shareholder can cast a total number of votes in the election equal to the number of shares owned, multiplied by the number of persons to be elected to the board. These votes can be cast all for one candidate or split up among the candidates as the shareholder sees fit.

Example: Shareholders A and B own 2,000 shares each and Shareholder C owns 1,000 shares. At the annual shareholders meeting, four candidates are nominated for election to a three-person board. Under normal voting rules with one share equal to one vote, C's candidate can always be outvoted by A's or B's choice. With cumulative voting, however, C is given 3,000 votes (A and C have 6,000 votes each). While still outnumbered, if C cumulates all 3,000 votes in favor of one candidate and A and B split their votes among the other three candidates, C has a chance of electing his or her nominee to the board.

Cumulative voting for directors is mandatory, by corporate statute or state constitution, in Arizona, California (in California, a shareholder must state the intention to cumulate votes prior to the vote at the annual meeting), Delaware, Hawaii, Kentucky, Missouri, Nebraska, North Dakota, South Dakota and West Virginia. The remaining states permit cumulative voting only if provided for, or not prohibited by, the Articles of Incorporation. Unless required, most small corporations do not use cumulative voting at the annual shareholders meeting to elect directors.

Step 14. Adjourn the Meeting

After all resolutions have been submitted to a vote of the directors or shareholders at a meeting, the chairperson should propose adjournment. If no further business is proposed and the motion carries, the meeting is adjourned.

If minutes were not prepared at the meeting, your next step is to prepare minutes to place in the corporate records book. We cover these and related forms in the next two chapters. For now, place all papers presented or drafted at the meeting in the folder for the meeting or directly in your corporate records book.

If a Meeting Is Adjourned With Unfinished Business

If a corporate meeting is carried over to another time when unfinished business can be concluded, the second meeting is referred to as the "adjourned meeting." When a meeting is adjourned to continue business at another time, we suggest you use common sense and send out notice for any meeting that is carried over more than a week or so from the original meeting, unless your Bylaws set a shorter standard for providing notice of the adjourned meeting. (For details, see Chapter 3, Section B, Step 5.)

CHAPTER 5

How to Prepare Written Minutes of Shareholders Meetings

In this chapter, we show you how to choose and use minutes forms to document actions taken at regular and special shareholders meetings. You will find sample minutes forms in this chapter, and ready-to-fill-in forms on your corporate records disk and in Appendix C. (Minutes for directors meetings are contained in Chapter 6.)

Our minutes forms are designed to document the most common procedures and actions taken at regular and special shareholders meetings, such as the election of directors at annual shareholder meetings. However, they do not include resolutions for the adoption of more specialized types of business that may be taken up at the meeting. To document these decisions, you will need to insert your own language. (See "How to Use Corporate Resolutions" sidebar, below.)

A. Preparing Minutes for Annual Shareholders Meetings

The first form we'll cover is the minutes form for annual shareholders meetings. Selecting and using this form is easy—just follow the instructions provided below. You'll see that all our minutes forms follow a consistent format; once you've used one, the rest will be even easier to use.

1. When Annual Minutes Should Be Prepared

There are no legal requirements on when minutes must be prepared. Common sense dictates that the minutes should, however, be prepared shortly after (within a few days or so of) the meeting being documented. If you wait longer, you may forget to prepare the minutes, or be unable to follow your notes or recollection as to the proposals made and votes taken at the meeting. Here are some suggestions.

If you hold a real meeting. If you are preparing minutes for a meeting that really takes place, as described in Chapter 4, the secretary will normally complete the minutes form after the meeting, based upon notes taken at the meeting. Or, if you wish, a draft of the form can be prepared before the meeting and completed during or after the meeting. Some people prefer to prepare the entire minutes form during the meeting, either by using a fill-in-the-blanks minutes form (see Appendix C) or by filling in the form with a computer at the meeting.

If you hold a paper meeting. To prepare minutes for a paper meeting that doesn't actually occur, follow our instructions in Chapter 7. The secretary normally prepares this minutes form whenever it's convenient; it need not be at the meeting date. He or she then distributes a copy to all shareholders for their approval as explained in Chapter 7, Section B, Step 5.

HOW TO USE CORPORATE RESOLUTIONS

Resolutions are inserted in annual or special minutes of shareholders meetings (or in written consent forms) to show formal approval of corporate legal, tax and other business decisions. We've included the standard language for the approval of business customarily handled at annual meetings of your shareholders in the minutes forms contained in this chapter. For special meetings, you will want to add your own language showing the approval of the particular business for which the special meeting was called.

It's easy to prepare resolutions to insert in your minutes forms after you do a few. We provide examples of using your own language in the special instructions to filling out minutes forms. If you want a ready-to-use collection of corporate resolutions that cover numerous items of business customarily approved by corporate shareholders, see Nolo's *Taking Care of Your Corporation, Vol. 2: Key Corporate Decisions Made Easy,* by Anthony Mancuso.

Most corporate resolutions stand on their own and do not require the preparation of additional documentation. However, some types of resolutions ratify or refer to additional backup agreements or paperwork, and you may wish to attach this supplementary material to your minutes. For example, if shareholders approve a resolution to make a loan to a director, you can prepare and attach a promissory note to your minutes. If you wish to prepare your own standard loan and business forms, you may be able to get copies from banks, real estate brokers, legal stationers, business law libraries or other sources. *Taking Care of Your Corporation, Vol. 2: Key Corporate Decisions Made Easy,* referred to above, provides various supplemental forms, such as promissory notes, shareholder buy-sell provisions and other information to help you take care of the business being approved by your shareholders.

2. How to Prepare Minutes of an Annual Shareholders Meeting

Below is a sample of the form you can use to prepare minutes of your annual shareholders meeting. This form specifically provides for the election of directors—the primary purpose of annual shareholders meetings. Prepare this form as you go through the sample form and special instructions that follow.

The filename for this form is SHARANNL, followed by a three-letter filename extension according to the version of the file. For example, Word users should select and use the SHARANNL.DOC file. (See Chapter 10 for information on selecting and using computer disk files.)

MINUTES OF THE ANNUAL MEETING OF SHAREHOLDERS OF

_____[name of corporation]_____ ❶

An annual meeting of the shareholders of the corporation was held on _____, 19___ ❷ at ___:___ __.M., at _[location of meeting]_, state of _____, for the purpose of electing the directors of the corporation and for the transaction of any other business that may properly come before the meeting, including ❸_____

_____.

❹_____ acted as chairperson, and _____ acted as secretary of the meeting.

The chairperson called the meeting to order.

The secretary announced that the meeting was called by _____ _____. ❺

The secretary announced that the meeting was held pursuant to notice, if and as required under the Bylaws of this corporation, or that notice had been waived by all shareholders entitled to receive notice under the Bylaws. Copies of any certificates of mailing of notice prepared by the secretary of the corporation and any written waivers signed by shareholders entitled to receive notice of this meeting were attached to these minutes by the secretary. ❻

The secretary announced that an alphabetical list of the names and numbers of shares held by all shareholders of the corporation was available and open to inspection by any person in attendance at the meeting. ❼

The secretary announced that there were present, in person or by proxy, representing a quorum of the shareholders, the following shareholders, proxyholders and shares: ❽

Name

Number of Shares

_____   _____

_____   _____

_____   _____

_____   _____

The secretary attached written proxy statements, executed by the appropriate shareholders, to these minutes for any shares listed above as held by a proxyholder.

The following persons were also present at the meeting: ❾

Name   Title

_____   _____

_____   _____

_____   _____

The secretary announced that the minutes of the __["annual," "special" or "regular"]__ meeting held on _____, 19___

☐ had been distributed prior to

☐ were distributed at

☐ were read at

the meeting. After discussion, a vote was taken and the minutes of the meeting were approved by the shares in attendance. ❿

The following annual and special reports were presented at the meeting by the following persons: ⓫

_____

_____

_____.

The chairperson announced that the next item of business was the nomination and election of the board of directors for another __["one-year" or other term]__ term of office. The following nominations were made and seconded: ⓬

Name(s) of Nominee(s)

_____

_____

_____

_____

     The secretary next took the votes of shareholders entitled to vote for the election of directors at the meeting, and, after counting the votes, announced that the following persons were elected to serve on the Board of Directors of this corporation for another term of office: **13**

Names of Board Members

_____

_____

_____

_____

_____

     On motion duly made and carried by the affirmative vote of ___["a majority of" or other vote requirement]___ shareholders in attendance at the meeting, the following resolutions were adopted by shareholders entitled to vote at the meeting: **14**

     There being no further business to come before the meeting, it was adjourned on motion duly made and carried.

15

_____

_____, Secretary

Special Instructions

❶ Most state statutes and Bylaws call for the annual election of directors by the shareholders. However, if your Bylaws require election less frequently, say every two years, then delete or change the word "annual" in the heading and text of the computer form (for example, by changing all occurrences of the word "annual" to "biennial"). Similarly, if your corporation has opted for a special staggered board with only a portion of the board elected each year, make a note of this in the first paragraph. If you use tear-out forms from Appendix C, cross out material as needed and neatly write in the changes.

❷ Complete the beginning of the first paragraph by inserting the date, time and place (street address, city and state) of the meeting. Shareholder meetings are usually held at the principal office of the corporation, although most Bylaws allow these meetings to be held anywhere within or outside the state.

❸ If you wish, list any matters, other than the election of directors, considered at the annual shareholders meeting. You are not legally required to do this, since the sentence already authorizes the transaction of any other business that may come before the meeting, but you may wish to do so anyway.

❹ Insert the name and title of the persons who acted as chairperson and secretary of the meeting. Often, corporate Bylaws specify who should act as chairperson of shareholder meetings. Normally this is the president or, in his or her absence, the vice-president or other director. Usually, the secretary of the corporation acts as secretary of all corporate meetings. In his or her absence, another director usually assumes this task.

Note. In the instructions for this form, we specify when we are referring to the secretary of the corporation. All other references are to refer to the secretary of the meeting. Again, normally the secretary of the corporation and the secretary of the meeting will be one and the same.

❺ This is an optional paragraph, which may be deleted or filled in as "not applicable" if you choose not to include it. Normally annual shareholders meetings are not officially "called," since they are already scheduled in the Bylaws. (See Chapter 3, Section B, Step 3, for a discussion of the legal requirements for calling corporate meetings.) If your corporation follows a different practice and you wish to show that the secretary of the corporation, or another officer, board member or a number of shareholders, called the meeting, include this paragraph. Indicate the name and title of each person who called the meeting.

❻ This paragraph states that each shareholder was given notice as required by your Bylaws or waived notice by signing a written waiver of notice form. For shareholder meetings, we generally recommend providing written notice prior to the meeting, since this is the best way to make sure each shareholder knows about the meeting well in advance and understands the nature of the proposals to be discussed there. If you own and run a closely-held corporation, you may be able to safely use waiver of notice forms. (For an overview of state notice requirements for shareholders meetings, see Chapter 3, Section B, Step 5.)

If notice was mailed to shareholders, attach to the minutes any Certificate of Mailing of notice or Acknowledgment of Receipt. (See Chapter 3, Section B, Steps 7 and 9b.) Attach any written waivers of notice for the meeting that were signed by shareholders. (See Chapter 7, Section B, Step 1, for instructions on preparing waiver of notice forms.)

Hand Out Waiver Forms to Save Time in Closely-held Corporations

Small corporations with only a few shareholders—who are almost guaranteed to attend meetings—sometimes decide to dispense with official premeeting notice formalities entirely, and, instead, informally notify all shareholders of the meeting. They then hand out written waiver of notice forms for each participant to sign. It's usually convenient to do so just prior to or at the meeting. This is perfectly legal and does no harm if you are sure each shareholder knows about the meeting and its purpose well in advance anyway. (See Chapter 7, Section B, Step 1, for instructions on preparing waiver forms.)

❼ This sentence restates a common legal requirement that an alphabetical list of shareholders be made available for inspection during the meeting. You can prepare a separate list as explained in Chapter 3, Section B, Step 4, or you can simply make your corporate record book available for inspection at the meeting if it includes a share register with a current listing of your shareholders and their shareholdings.

❽ List the names of the shareholders present at the meeting. To the right of each name, show the number of shares owned by the shareholder.

If shares are represented by proxy, list the proxyholder's name on the left, followed by the words "proxyholder for" and the name of the shareholder. Show the number of shares held by the proxyholder under the column at the right. (See Chapter 3, Section B, Step 8, for a discussion of when to use and how to prepare proxy forms for shareholders.)

Example: Victor Lewis attends the meeting with a written proxy signed by Margaret Billings to vote 1,000 shares for Margaret. The secretary fills out the minutes as follows:

Name	*Number of Shares*
Victor Lewis, proxyholder for Margaret Billings	*1,000*

If any proxyholders attend a meeting, attach to the minutes a written proxy statement dated and signed by the shareholder whose shares are represented by proxy. Proxy forms are included on the corporate disk and in Appendix C, as explained in step-by-step instructions in Chapter 3, Section B, Step 8.

Quorum Requirements Reminder

Most Bylaws require that a majority of the voting shares of the corporation attend the meeting for a quorum to be in attendance. (See Chapter 4, Step 8.)

Example: Bioflex Weight Training Systems, Inc. holds a shareholders meeting. The corporation's Bylaws require a majority of the 2,000 issued shares as a quorum for shareholders meetings. Since the following shareholders holding 1,500 shares show up for the meeting, a quorum is present and the meeting can be convened:

Name	*Number of Shares*
Robert Newquist	*1,000*
Rebecca Michigan	*300*
Samuel Thatcher	*200*

❾ Specify any additional persons, other than the chairperson and secretary of the meeting, who attend the meeting but do not count towards a quorum. For example, if informational reports are to be made to the shareholders by non-shareholder corporate officers, staff or committee members, they, of course, will also be in attendance, as well as possibly the corporation's accountant or legal consultant.

❿ It is customary, though not legally necessary, for participants at an annual meeting to approve the minutes of the previous shareholders meeting. This prior meeting may have been last year's annual meeting or a special meeting of shareholders called during the year. Mostly, this formality of approving prior minutes is undertaken to remind everyone of any special business approved at the last meeting and to allow any objections prior to placing a formal copy of the minutes in the corporate records book.

If you decide to follow this formality and wish to save time, you can send copies of the minutes of the last meeting to each participant to read prior to the meeting, as explained in Chapter 7, Section B, Steps 3-5. Otherwise, distribute copies of the minutes at the current meeting or have the secretary read or summarize them. Then ask for a voice approval. Normally, the prior meeting's minutes are routinely approved, but if there are objections, you will need to work them out before approving the minutes. You may do this either by making appropriate corrections to the prior minutes or by obtaining a majority vote to approve the minutes over the objection of one or more shareholders.

Fill in the blanks as shown in the sample form to indicate the method of distributing or announcing the minutes of the prior meeting to shareholders. If you choose not to address minutes, simply delete this reference or fill in "not applicable."

Use Written Approval Forms to Save Time or Obtain Specific Consent to Past Decisions

Written minute approval forms can be sent out to shareholders along with the prior minutes before the meeting to obtain signed approval of those minutes. Using this form can save time and has the added advantage of providing signed consent to previous decisions reached at that meeting. This may be helpful, for example, if some shareholders did not attend the last meeting and you wish to have a record of their approval of important decisions reached at that meeting. (How to prepare a written Approval of Corporate Minutes form is covered in Chapter 7, Section B, Step 3.)

If you use an Approval of Corporate Minutes form to obtain written approval of minutes of a prior meeting, change this paragraph in the current annual minutes form to read as follows:

The secretary announced that the minutes of the   [regular, annual or special shareholders]   meeting held on   [date] , 19__, had been distributed prior to the meeting and that each shareholder had returned to the secretary of the corporation a signed statement showing approval of the minutes of the prior meeting. [Delete the next sentence in the form showing a vote taken at the meeting.]

⓫ As explained in Chapter 4, Step 10, you may wish to present annual or special reports at your meeting. For example, the president may present an annual operating report and the treasurer may summarize the past year's financial gains or losses. List a description of the reports given, such as "treasurer's report of sales," along with the name and title of the presenter. Attach any written copies of reports to your minutes.

⓬ Here you take care of the main business of the annual shareholders meeting—the election (or re-election) of the directors of your corporation for another term of office. Indicate the term of office of the board in the first blank. Most Bylaws provide for a one-year (annual) term of office, although occasionally, Bylaws specify a longer term. Under "Name of Nominee(s)," fill in the names of all nominees who are to be voted upon by the share-holders. Many small corporations simply nominate (and re-elect) each member of the current board for another term of office. But check your Bylaws to be sure. Modern corporate statutes allow corporations to provide for a classified or staggered board in their Bylaws. Typically, this means that the board is broken down—or classified—into two or more sections, with the elections for each section occurring on alternate years.

Example: Quark Corp. has a nine-member board, and its Bylaws provide for one-third of the board to be re-elected every three years. At each annual share-holders meeting, one-third of the classified board is re-elected to another three-year term.

🔟 In these blanks, indicate the persons who are elected to serve on the board for another term.

There are different ways ballots can be counted. Corporations usually use voice vote or written ballot. In some circumstances, your Articles or Bylaws may call for cumulative voting procedures. (We discuss shareholder voting rules in Chapter 4, Step 13b.)

Normal voting procedures. Most corporations elect directors by voice vote or written ballot, and elect those nominees who receive the most votes.

Example: Ten shareholders holding 100 shares apiece vote for three of five nominees to a three-person board (each shareholder may cast 100 votes in favor of each of three candidates). The results are as follows:

	Number of Votes Cast	*Result in Favor of Candidate*
Nominee 1	*1,000*	*Elected*
Nominee 2	*1,000*	*Elected*
Nominee 3	*500*	*Elected*
Nominee 4	*300*	*Not Elected*
Nominee 5	*200*	*Not Elected*

In the above example, Nominees 1 and 2 received the votes of all ten share-holders, while Nominees 3, 4 and 5 received the votes of five, three and two shareholders respectively. The three candidates receiving the largest number of votes, Nominees 1, 2 and 3, are elected to the board.

Cumulative voting procedures. There is another way of electing directors—namely, by cumulative voting procedures. Your Articles of Incorporation or Bylaws should state whether you are required to, are prohibited from, or have the option to use cumulative voting procedures when electing directors of the corporation. Often, the Bylaws state that cumulative voting must be used to elect directors at the annual shareholders meeting if any shareholder makes a request for cumulative voting prior to the commencement of voting for directors.

Cumulative voting differs from standard plurality voting in that a shareholder is given a total number of votes equal to his or her shares times the number of directors to be elected. The shareholder may vote all votes for one candidate—this is known as cumulating his or her votes—or may split them up among two or more candidates.

Example: Using the same ten shareholders and five nominees as in the previous example, under cumulative voting each shareholder is given a total of 500 votes to cast for one or more directors. This means that any one shareholder has a better chance of tipping the scales in favor of one candidate since he or she is no longer limited to voting a maximum of 100 votes for a particular candidate. Of course, a shareholder will lose a chance to vote for any other candidates by casting all votes for one nominee. In fact, this is the purpose of cumulative voting, and a reason why it is used in larger corporations: it gives minority shareholders a better shot at electing a candidate to the board, despite the voting power of the majority shareholders. (For a further discussion of cumulative voting rules, see Chapter 4, Step 13b.)

❹ Many small corporations use their annual shareholders meeting simply to re-elect directors and to provide progress reports to the shareholders regarding corporate operations and profits. If you decide to present other proposals for a vote by shareholders at your annual meeting, such as a ratification by shareholders of an amendment to the corporation's Articles or Bylaws, insert one or more resolutions that describe the matter approved in this space.

You don't need to use fancy or legal language for your resolution; just describe as specifically as you can the transaction or matter approved by your shareholders in a short, concise statement. Normally, resolutions start with a preamble of the following sort: "The shareholders resolved that…" but this is not required.

Following are some sample shareholder resolutions.

Example 1 (Amendment of Articles): "The shareholders ratified a board of directors resolution adding the following new articles to the corporation's Articles of Incorporation: [language of new article]."

Example 2 (Amendment of Bylaws): "The shareholders approved an amendment to the Bylaws of the corporation. The text of the changed Bylaws is as follows: [language of amended Bylaws]."

If you have trouble finding or drafting a resolution, or if the matter has important legal or tax consequences, you may wish to turn to a lawyer or accountant for help. (See Chapter 9.)

Nolo's *Taking Care of Your Corporation, Vol. 2: Key Corporate Decisions Made Easy*, by Anthony Mancuso, contains ready-to-use resolutions for common corporate legal, tax, financial and business transactions. Also included in the tear-out and computer disk forms are backup forms, such as promissory notes, employment contracts, shareholder buy-sell provisions, and legal and tax information to help you take care of the business approved by your shareholders at meetings.

⓯ This concluding adjournment paragraph and signature line should appear at the very end of your minutes after any resolutions. Fill in the name of the secretary of the meeting under the signature line.

After obtaining the signature of the secretary, file the completed minutes in your corporate records book together with all attachments.

If you prepared a separate meeting folder for the annual meeting (see Chapter 3, Section B, Step 1), now is the time to transfer all forms and attachments related to the meeting from the folder to your corporate records book.

B. Preparing Minutes of Special Shareholders Meetings

Now let's look at the form to use to document the proceedings of special meetings of your shareholders—meetings called during the year for the purpose of approving one or more items of special shareholder business.

1. When Special Minutes Should Be Prepared

Unlike regular or annual meetings of shareholders that are scheduled in your Bylaws, special meetings are called during the year to discuss and vote upon special items of corporate business presented for approval to the shareholders.

Special meetings of shareholders are called and held less frequently than any other kind of corporate meeting. The reason, of course, is that the great majority of corporate business is conducted by the directors, not the shareholders. (See Chapter 2, Sections B9 and B10.)

Mostly, meetings of this sort are held if required under state law to ratify action taken by the board of directors or to obtain shareholder approval of a matter on which it can act independently (such as the amendment of Bylaws). Generally, state corporate statutes only require the approval by shareholders of important structural changes to the corporation or of matters in which the directors have a direct financial interest. For example, a special shareholders meeting might be called to ratify an amendment to the Articles, the authorization or issuance of additional shares of stock or a dissolution of the corporation. It may also be called to approve loans, guarantees and other business favorable to the financial interests of one or more members of the board of directors.

Generally, special meetings of shareholders are called by the directors to ask for ratification of a decision already made by the board, such as an amendment of the Articles or Bylaws of the corporation, or another major structural change to the corporation. In other words, most of the groundwork for preparing these minutes, including the drafting of resolutions to present to the special shareholders meeting, will already have been done.

Quorum Requirements Reminder

Your Bylaws should state any special shareholder quorum or vote requirements for the ratification of amendments or approval of other business by shareholders at shareholders meetings.

2. How to Prepare Minutes of a Special Shareholders Meeting

Below is the minutes form to use to document actions taken at a special meeting of your shareholders. This form is similar to the annual shareholders meeting form presented in Section A2, above, but eliminates the election of directors as an item on the agenda at the meeting.

Provide Notice or Waivers Reminder

Remember to call and provide notice for all special shareholder meetings as provided in your Bylaws (Chapter 3, Section B, Steps 3-5). Or, in the alternative, have each shareholder sign a written waiver of notice form prior to the meeting (Chapter 7, Section B, Step 1). Each notice or waiver of notice form should state the specific purpose(s) of the special shareholders meeting since state law usually prohibits the transaction of any business not specified in the notice or waiver of notice for the special shareholders meeting.

The filename for this form is SHARSPCL, followed by a three-letter filename extension according to the version of the file. For example, Word users should select and use the SHARSPCL.DOC file. (See Chapter 10 for information on selecting and using computer disk files.)

MINUTES OF SPECIAL MEETING OF SHAREHOLDERS OF

_____[name of corporation]_____

A special meeting of the shareholders of the corporation was held on

_____, 19___ at ___:___ __.M., at ❶ __[name of corporation]__, state of

_____, for the purpose(s) of ❷

_____

_____.

❸ _____ acted as chairperson, and

_____ acted as secretary of the meeting.

The chairperson called the meeting to order.

The secretary announced that the meeting was called by

_____.❹

The secretary announced that the meeting was held pursuant to notice, if and as required under the Bylaws of this corporation, or that notice had been waived by all shareholders entitled to receive notice under the Bylaws. Copies of any certificates of mailing of notice prepared by the secretary of the corporation and any written waivers signed by shareholders entitled to receive notice of this meeting were attached to these minutes by the secretary. ❺

The secretary announced that an alphabetical list of the names and numbers of shares held by all shareholders of the corporation was available and open to inspection by any person in attendance at the meeting.❻

The secretary announced that there were present, in person or by proxy, representing a quorum of the shareholders, the following shareholders, proxyholders and shares:❼

Name   Number of Shares

_____   _____

_____   _____

_____   _____

The secretary attached written proxy statements, executed by the appropriate shareholders, to these minutes for any shares listed above as held by a proxyholder.

The following persons were also present at the meeting:❽

Name	Title
_____	_____
_____	_____
_____	_____
_____	_____

The secretary announced that the minutes of the ___["annual," "regular" or "special" shareholders]___ meeting held on _____, 19___

☐ had been distributed prior to

☐ were distributed at

☐ were read at

the meeting. After discussion, a vote was taken and the minutes of the meeting were approved by the shares in attendance.❾

The following reports were presented at the meeting by the following persons: ❿

_____

_____

_____

_____

_____

_____ .

On motion duly made and carried by the affirmative vote of ___["a majority of" or other vote requirement]___ shareholders in attendance at the meeting, the following resolutions were adopted by shareholders entitled to vote at the meeting: ⓫

There being no further business to come before the meeting, it was adjourned on motion duly made and carried.

⓬

_____

_____, Secretary

Special Instructions

❶ Insert the date, time and place (street address, city and state) of the meeting. Shareholders meetings are usually held at the principal office of the corporation, although most Bylaws allow these meetings to be held anywhere.

❷ List the specific purpose(s) for which this special shareholders meeting was called. A similar statement of purpose(s) should have been included in your notice (Chapter 3, Section B, Step 5) or waiver of notice form (Chapter 7, Section B, Step 1) used for the meeting.

Sample statements of purpose of special meeting include:

- "ratifying an amendment to the Articles of Incorporation that provides for the creation of a new class of shares," or

- "approving an amendment to the Bylaws of the corporation that increases the minimum quorum requirement for shareholders meetings."

❸ Insert the name and title of the persons who acted as chairperson and secretary of the meeting. Bylaws typically provide that the president or chairperson of the Board presides at, and the corporate secretary acts as secretary of, meetings of shareholders.

Note. In the instructions for this form, we specify when we are referring to the secretary of the corporation. All other references are to the secretary of the meeting. Again, normally the secretary of the corporation and the secretary of the meeting will be one and the same.

❹ Indicate the person or persons who called the special meeting of shareholders, along with each person's title. Typically, Bylaws and state law allow the board of directors, the president or a minimum of 10% of the shares to call a special meeting of shareholders. (See Chapter 3, Section B, Step 3, and check your Bylaws.)

❺ Proper notice or waiver of notice is particularly important for special shareholders meetings. After all, you don't want an uninformed shareholder to complain later and challenge a decision made at a special shareholders meeting. This paragraph states that each shareholder was given notice as required by your Bylaws or waived notice by signing a written waiver form.

Hand Out Waiver Forms to Save Time in Closely-held Corporations

Small corporations with only a few shareholders—who are almost guaranteed to attend meetings—sometimes decide to dispense with official pre-meeting notice formalities entirely, and, instead, informally notify all shareholders of the meeting. They usually hand out written waiver of notice forms just prior to or at a meeting for each participant to sign. This is perfectly legal and does no harm if you are sure each shareholder knows about the meeting and its purpose well in advance anyway. (See Chapter 7, Section B, Step 1, for instructions on preparing the waiver of notice form.)

If notice was mailed to shareholders, attach to the minutes any Certificate of Mailing of notice or Acknowledgments of r=Receipt. (See Chapter 3, Section B, Steps 7 and 9b.) Attach any written waivers of notice for the meeting that were signed by shareholders. (See Chapter 7, Section B, Step 1, for instructions on preparing waiver of notice forms.)

❻ This sentence restates a common requirement that an alphabetical list of shareholders be made available for inspection during the meeting. You can prepare a separate list as explained in Chapter 3, Section B, Step 4, or you can simply make your corporate records book available for inspection if it includes a share register with a current listing of your shareholders and their shareholdings.

❼ List the names of the shareholders present at the meeting. To the right of each name, show the number of shares owned by the shareholder.

If shares are represented by proxy, list the proxyholder's name on the left, followed by the words "proxyholder for" and the name of the shareholder. Show the number of shares held by the proxyholder under the column at the right. (See Chapter 3, Section B, Step 8, for a discussion of when to use and how to prepare proxy forms for shareholders.)

Example: Victor Lewis attends the meeting with a written proxy signed by Margaret Billings to vote 1,000 shares for Margaret. The secretary fills out the minutes as follows:

Name	*Number of Shares*
Victor Lewis, proxyholder for Margaret Billings	*1,000*

If any proxyholders attend a meeting, attach to the minutes a written proxy statement dated and signed by the shareholder. Proxy forms, included on the corporate records disk and Appendix C, are discussed in step-by-step instructions in Chapter 3, Section B, Step 8.

Quorum Requirements Reminder

Most Bylaws require that a majority of the voting shares of the corporation attend the meeting for a quorum to be in attendance. (See Chapter 4, Step 8.)

Example: Bioflex Weight Training Systems, Inc. holds a shareholders meeting. The corporation's Bylaws require a majority of the 2,000 issued shares as a quorum for shareholders meetings. Since the following shareholders holding 1,500 shares show up for the meeting, a quorum is present and the meeting can be convened:

Name	*Number of Shares*
Robert Newquist	*1,000*
Rebecca Michigan	*300*
Samuel Thatcher	*200*

❽ Specify any additional persons (other than the chairperson and secretary of the meeting) who attend the meeting but do not count towards a quorum. If reports are to be submitted to the shareholders by non-shareholder corporate officers, staff or committee members, they, of course, will be in attendance, as well as, possibly, the corporation's accountant or legal consultant.

❾ It is customary, though not legally necessary, for participants at a shareholders meeting to approve the minutes of the previous meeting. The prior meeting may have been an annual or special shareholders meeting. Mostly, this formality is undertaken to remind everyone of any special business approved at the last meeting and to allow any objections prior to placing a formal copy of the minutes in the corporate records book.

If you decide to follow this formality and wish to save time, you can send copies of the minutes of the last meeting to each participant to read prior to the meeting, as explained in Chapter 3, Section B, Steps 3-5. Otherwise, distribute copy of the minutes or have the secretary read or summarize them. Then ask for a voice approval. Normally, the minutes are routinely approved. If there are suggestions or corrections, you will need to work them out before voting to approve the minutes. You may do this by making appropriate corrections to the prior minutes. In the rare event this proves impossible, you'll need to obtain a majority vote to approve the minutes over the objection of one or more shareholders.

Fill in the blanks as shown to indicate the method of distributing or announcing the minutes of the prior meeting to shareholders.

Use Written Approval Forms to Save Time or Obtain Specific Consent to Past Decisions

Written minutes approval forms can be sent out to shareholders along with the prior minutes before the meeting to obtain written approval of the prior minutes. Using this form can save time and has the added advantage of providing signed consent to previous decisions reached at meetings. This may be helpful, for example, if some shareholders did not attend the last meeting and you wish to have a record of their approval of important decisions reached at the previous meeting. How to prepare a written

Approval of Corporate Minutes form is covered in Chapter 7, Section B, Step 3.

If you use an Approval of Corporate Minutes form to obtain written approval to the minutes of a prior meeting, change this paragraph in the current minutes to read as follows:

The secretary announced that the minutes of the   [regular, annual or special shareholders]   meeting held on   [date] , 19__, had been distributed prior to the meeting and that each shareholder had returned to the secretary of the corporation a signed statement showing approval of the minutes of the prior meeting. [Delete the next sentence in the form showing a vote taken at the meeting.]

❿ If reports are presented to shareholders by officers, staff, outside accountants, lawyers or others at the meeting, specify the nature of each report, such as "treasurer's report of sales." Include the name and title of each person making or submitting a report. Attach to your minutes copies of any written reports passed out to participants at the meeting.

⓫ Here you take care of the main business of a special shareholders meeting—the passage of one or more specific resolutions by the shareholders in attendance at the meeting. In the blank, insert the vote requirement for the resolution(s) that follow(s) this paragraph. As explained in Chapter 4, Section B, Step 13b, shareholder resolutions normally must be passed by a majority of those attending and entitled to vote at a meeting—check your Bylaws. If you pass a resolution that requires a different vote requirement than other resolutions under your Bylaws, you should precede the text of the resolution with a statement that the resolution was passed by the appropriate number or percentage of votes.

In the space below the paragraph, insert one or more resolutions that describe the specific legal, tax, financial or other items of business voted upon and approved at the meeting. Normally, as explained in Chapter 2, shareholders will be asked to ratify a board decision, such as an amendment of the Articles already approved by the directors, although they can act independently to approve certain matters on their own, for example the amendment of Bylaws.

You don't need to use fancy or legal language for your resolution; just describe as specifically as you can the transaction or matter approved by your shareholders in a short, concise statement. Normally, resolutions start with a preamble of the following sort: "The shareholders resolved that…" but this is not required.

Following are some sample resolutions of shareholders.

Example 1 (Amendment of Articles): "The shareholders ratified a board of directors resolution adding the following new articles to the corporation's Articles of Incorporation [language of new article]."

Example 2 (Amendment of Bylaws): "The shareholders approved an amendment to the Bylaws of the corporation. The text of the changed Bylaws is as follows: [language of amended Bylaws]."

If you have trouble finding or drafting a resolution, or if the matter has important legal or tax consequences, you may wish to turn to a lawyer or accountant for help. (See Chapter 9.)

Nolo's *Taking Care of Your Corporation, Vol. 2: Key Corporate Decisions Made Easy,* by Anthony Mancuso, contains ready-to-use resolutions for common corporate legal, tax, financial and business transactions. Also included in the tear-out and computer disk forms are backup forms, such as promissory notes, employment contracts, shareholder buy-sell provisions, and legal and tax information to help you take care of the business approved by your shareholders at meetings.

⓬ This concluding adjournment paragraph and signature line should appear at the very end of your minutes, after any resolutions. Fill in the name of the secretary of the meeting under the signature line. After obtaining the signature of the secretary, file the completed minutes in your corporate records book together with all attachments.

If you prepared a separate meeting folder for the special meeting (see Chapter 3, Section B, Step 1), now is the time to transfer all forms and attachments related to the meeting from your folder to your corporate records book.

CHAPTER 6

How to Prepare Written Minutes of Directors Meetings

The key to documenting the actions of your board of directors is to prepare accurate minutes of your regular and special meetings. In this chapter we show you how to prepare and use minutes forms for directors meetings. (To fill in minutes forms for annual and special meetings of shareholders, see Chapter 5.)

At this point, we assume you have followed the preliminary steps set out in Chapter 3 to call, provide notice and get ready for your upcoming directors meeting.

Minutes of directors meetings are most often prepared by the corporate secretary shortly after the meeting based upon notes taken at the meeting. But you can opt to prepare minutes during the meeting, by filling in a draft minutes form from Appendix C or a computer-generated copy. You may also consider using a computer at the meeting to fill in the form.

If You're Holding a Paper Meeting

You can also use the minutes forms set out in this chapter to prepare minutes for a meeting that occurs only on paper. This paper meeting procedure works well for small businesses with only a few directors, who agree on all major points but who want to prepare a professional-looking record of their actions. (See Chapter 7.)

SKIPPING MINUTES ALTOGETHER

Corporations with very few directors who agree as to all major points may not want to deal with meetings or minutes forms at all. It's legal to have directors take action by unanimous written consent without a meeting and without formal minutes, as explained in Chapter 8.

But even with a tiny corporation, there is a downside. Written consents provide minimal documentation of corporate action and may not be as official-looking to the IRS and other agencies.

The minutes forms covered in this chapter contain the language necessary to document standard items normally dealt with at annual and special meetings of your directors. For example, the annual meeting minutes form shows acceptance by the directors of their election for another term, as well as other routine items of business, such as establishing that a quorum is present and approving the minutes of prior meetings.

At some annual and all special meetings of directors, you will want your directors to approve items of business not specifically listed in our forms. For example, at a special meeting of directors, you might want to authorize a bank loan or the purchase of real property. To document any of these more specialized actions, you will need to insert the necessary resolution in your minutes showing the acceptance of these terms by the board. Our instructions to the forms explain that providing your own language for each resolution should take but a few minutes. (See "How to Use Corporate Resolutions" sidebar, below.)

HOW TO USE CORPORATE RESOLUTIONS

Resolutions are inserted in annual or special minutes of directors meetings (or in written consent forms) to show formal approval of corporate legal, tax and other business decisions. We've included the standard language for the approval of business customarily handled at annual meetings of your board in the minutes forms contained in this chapter. For special meetings, you will want to add your own language showing the approval of the particular business for which the special meeting was called.

It's easy to prepare resolutions to insert in your minute forms after you do a few. We provide examples of using your own language in the special instructions to filling out minutes forms. If you want a ready-to-use collection of corporate resolutions that cover numerous items of business customarily approved by corporate directors, see Nolo's *Taking Care of Your Corporation, Vol. 2: Key Corporate Decisions Made Easy,* by Anthony Mancuso.

Most corporate resolutions stand on their own and do not require the preparation of additional documentation. For example, a board resolution declaring a dividend or approving a bonus does not normally refer to or require the preparation of additional documents. However, some types of resolutions ratify or refer to additional backup agreements or paperwork, and you may wish to attach this supplementary material to your minutes. For example, if the board approves the terms of an employment contract entered into with an officer, a copy of the completed contract can be attached to the resolution. If you wish to prepare your own standard loan and business forms, you may be able to get copies from banks, real estate brokers, legal stationers, business law libraries or other sources. *Taking Care of Your Corporation, Vol. 2: Key Corporate Decisions Made Easy*, referred to above, provides various supplemental forms, such as promissory notes, employment contracts and other information to help you take care of the business being approved by your board.

A. Choosing the Correct Minutes Form for a Directors Meeting

We've already touched upon the basic differences between annual (sometimes called "regular") and special meetings of the board of directors. (See
Chapters 2 and 4 for more information.) Here's a recap of a few essential
points:

When to hold annual directors meetings. The annual directors meeting is
normally held on the same day or shortly after the annual shareholders
meeting. At this meeting, the directors accept their election to the board by
the shareholders and transact any additional business brought before the
meeting.

*Example: All officers, directors and shareholders attend the annual sharehold-
ers meeting of WIZ-E-WIG Computer Graphics, Inc. Reports are given by the
corporate president and treasurer, summarizing the business operations and
results of the preceding year and outlining plans for the future. The shareholders
then re-elect the five-person board for another one-year term. Next, the shareholders leave, and the newly constituted board stays behind. First, the board
members accept their re-election to the board; then they discuss business plans for
the upcoming year. Of course, if corporate shareholders also serve as board
members when the shareholders meeting ends, the shareholders simply don their
directors hats and reconvene to transact business of the annual directors meeting.*

What is covered in annual directors meetings. Routine items of business
which are typically taken up at the annual directors meeting include the
appointment of officers for another year by the directors, the announcement
of important salary increases or bonuses approved for the past or upcoming
year, and reports of past or upcoming corporate business of importance to
the directors. We include each of these items of business in the annual
minutes form in Section B. Our annual minutes form also contains space to
add special resolutions to show the completion of any non-routine business
taken up and approved at the annual meeting, such as the approval of a
401(k) profit-sharing plan.

When to hold special meetings. Special meetings of directors are called
during the year to discuss and approve specific items of corporate business
as the need arises. In fairly rare circumstances, a special meeting of shareholders is called shortly after the special directors meeting to obtain shareholder ratification of the director decision. For example, this would be

appropriate if a structural change to the corporation is needed; that requires amending the Articles of Incorporation (to authorize a new class of shares).

Remember to Give Advance Notice

Your Bylaws should specify the date and time of your annual (or regular) meeting of directors. As we emphasize in Chapter 3, Section B, Step 5, it is important to provide directors with notice of upcoming meetings well in advance of the proposed meeting date. This is particularly important for special meetings of directors that are not scheduled in the corporation's Bylaws—you want to make sure to inform all directors that a special meeting has been called by the president, a board member or another person authorized to do so.

B. Preparing Minutes for Annual Directors Meetings

Below is a sample annual minutes form for an annual directors meeting. For help in completing it, refer to the special instructions which immediately follow this annual meeting form.

The filename for this form is DIRANNL, followed by a three-letter filename extension according to the version of the file. For example, Word users should select and use the DIRANNL.DOC file. (See Chapter 10 for information on selecting and using the computer disk files.)

MINUTES OF THE ANNUAL MEETING OF DIRECTORS OF

_____[name of corporation]_____

An annual meeting of the directors of the corporation was held on
_____, 19___ at ___:___ __.M., at ❶ __[location of meeting]__, state of
_____, for the purpose of reviewing the prior year's
business, discussing corporate operations for the upcoming year, and for the transaction of any
other business that may properly come before the meeting, including ❷

_____

_____

_____.

_____ acted as chairperson, and
_____ acted as secretary of the meeting. ❸

The chairperson called the meeting to order.

The secretary announced that the meeting was called by
_____. ❹

The secretary announced that the meeting was held pursuant to notice, if and as required
under the Bylaws of this corporation, or that notice had been waived by all directors entitled to
receive notice under the Bylaws. Copies of any certificates of mailing of notice prepared by the
secretary of the corporation and any written waivers signed by directors entitled to receive notice of
this meeting were attached to these minutes by the secretary. ❺

The secretary announced that the following directors were present at the meeting: ❻

Name of Director

_____

_____

_____

_____

The above directors, having been elected to serve on the board for another __["one-year" or other term]__ term by the shareholders at an annual meeting of shareholders held on _____, 19___, accepted their positions on the board. The secretary then announced that the presence of these directors at the meeting represented a quorum of the board of directors as defined in the Bylaws of this corporation.

The following persons were also present at the meeting: ❼

Name   Title

_____   _____

_____   _____

_____   _____

_____   _____

☐ The secretary announced that the minutes of the __["annual" "regular" or "special" directors]__ meeting held on _____, 19___

☐ had been distributed prior to

☐ were distributed at

☐ were read at

the meeting. After discussion, a vote was taken and the minutes of the meeting were approved by the directors in attendance. ❽

The following reports were presented at the meeting by the following persons: ❾

_____

_____

_____.

The chairperson announced that the next item of business was the appointment of the officers and of standing committee members of the corporation to another __["one-year" or other term]__ term of office. After discussion, the following persons were appointed to serve in the following capacities as officers, committee members or in other roles in the service of the corporation for the upcoming year: ❿

Name   Title

_____   _____

_____   _____

_____   _____

_____   _____

    The next item of business was the determination of compensation or fringe benefits to be paid or awarded for services rendered the corporation by employees and staff. After discussion, the following employee compensation amounts were approved by the board to be paid for the upcoming fiscal year to the following employees of the corporation: ⓫

Name   Type and Amount of
                                                        Compensation or Benefit

_____   _____

_____   _____

_____   _____

_____   _____

_____   _____

    On motion duly made and carried by the affirmative vote of __["a majority of" or other vote requirement]__ directors in attendance at the meeting, the following resolutions were adopted by directors entitled to vote at the meeting: ⓬

    There being no further business to come before the meeting, it was adjourned on motion duly made and carried.

⓭

_____

_____, Secretary

Special Instructions

❶ Your Bylaws should specify the date, time and place of annual directors meetings (also called "regular" directors meetings). Most annual meetings are held at the principal office of the corporation, although any meeting place, whether within or outside the state, typically is permitted under corporate Bylaws and state corporate statutes.

❷ Even though this paragraph includes the approval of "the transaction of any other business that may properly come before the meeting," it makes sense to mention all special resolutions that you plan to present to the annual meeting and which you will insert at the end of your minutes form. (See Special Instruction 12, below.[1]) Do not mention standard agenda items and matters of routine business here, such as acceptance by the board of their elected positions or the reappointment of officers at the annual meeting, which are already built into the minute form.

❸ Insert the name and title of the persons who acted as chairperson and secretary of the meeting. Normally, the president acts as chairperson of the board, and the secretary of the corporation usually acts as secretary of corporate meetings. Under most Bylaws, anyone may serve in any one these capacities, so you are normally free to appoint another director, officer or staff person to take over if the person normally delegated to perform one of these tasks is absent.

Note. In the instructions for this form, we specify when we are referring to the secretary of the corporation. All other references are to the secretary of the meeting. Again, normally the secretary of the corporation and the secretary of the meeting will be one and the same.

❹ This is an optional paragraph, which may be deleted or filled in as "not applicable" if you choose not to include it. Normally annual directors meetings are not called, since they are scheduled in the Bylaws. (See Chapter 3, Section B, Step 3a, for a discussion of the legal requirements for calling corporate meetings.) If your corporation follows a different practice, you may wish to show the corporate secretary as the person who called the annual directors meeting.

---

[1]As explained in Chapter 3, Section B, Step 5, notice of regular meetings is normally not required for annual director meetings, and the directors may normally transact any business at the meeting whether or not it was stated in a notice or waiver of notice for the meeting.

❺ This statement indicates that notice, if required, was given to or waived by each director. As explained in Chapter 3, Section B, Step 5, although notice is usually not legally required for annual directors meetings under most Bylaws, we suggest that you do provide it or have each director sign a waiver of notice form. After all, if you are going to the trouble of holding (or at least documenting) an annual meeting, why not make sure everyone knows about the meeting? If notice is mailed to directors, your corporate secretary may wish to prepare and attach a Certificate of Mailing of notice to the minutes. (See Chapter 3, Section B, Step 9b.) Also attach any written waivers of notice for the meeting that have been signed by directors. (See Chapter 7, Section B, Step 1, to prepare the waiver of notice form.)

❻ List the names of the directors present at the meeting. There must be a sufficient number of directors present to represent a quorum for a directors meeting under your Bylaws. (See Chapter 4, Step 8a.)

Before announcing the achievement of a quorum in the next paragraph, the minutes indicate that all board members accepted their election to the board for another year. Most corporations hold their annual meeting of shareholders just before the annual board meeting to re-elect the board to another one-year term. Fill in the date of the annual meeting of shareholders in the blank provided. If your directors were not re-elected at the recent annual shareholders meeting (for example, if they are elected biennially), insert "not applicable" in this blank.

Example: The Bylaws of Supple Shoe Corp. authorize five directors and specify that a quorum for directors meetings consists of a majority of the full board. Three directors, therefore, must attend the meeting in order for a quorum to be in attendance. If less than three attend the meeting, it must be adjourned until another date and time when a quorum can attend. (For the rules on providing notice of the adjourned meeting, see Chapter 3, Section B, Step 5.)

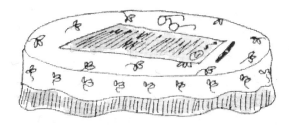

Directors Normally Can't Act by Proxy

Corporate statutes normally allow shareholders, but not directors, to designate another person to vote at a meeting by proxy. Even if allowed, letting someone vote for a board member is risky: the board member could be held liable for another person's negligent or ill-advised board decisions. Bottom line for board of directors members: directors should take an active, personal interest in the decisions discussed and voted upon at board meetings, or consider resigning from the board.

❼ Specify any additional persons (other than the chairperson and secretary of the meeting) who attend the meeting but do not count towards a quorum. If reports are to be submitted to the directors, additional corporate officers, staff or committee members may be in attendance, as well as the corporation's accountant or legal consultant.

List the president and treasurer here if you plan to follow our format in Special Instruction 9, below, indicating that these officers presented annual reports to the board. Also list the names of any other officers or committee members who will report to the board at the meeting.

❽ It is customary, though not legally necessary, for participants at an annual meeting to approve the minutes of the previous directors meeting. Mostly this formality is undertaken to remind everyone of any special business approved at the last meeting and to allow any objections prior to placing a formal copy of the minutes in the corporate records book.

If you decide to follow this formality and wish to save time, you may send copies of the minutes of the last meeting to each participant to read prior to the meeting, as explained in Chapter 7, Section B, Steps 3-5. Otherwise, distribute copies of the minutes or have the secretary read or summarize them. Then ask for voice approval. Normally, the minutes are routinely approved, but if there are objections, you will need to work them out before approving the minutes. You may make appropriate corrections to the minutes or obtain a majority vote to approve the minutes over the objection of one or more directors. Fill in the blanks as shown to indicate the method of distributing or announcing the minutes of the prior meeting to directors. If you choose not to address prior minutes at your meeting, either delete this entire paragraph or fill in "not applicable."

Use Written Approval Forms to Save Time or Obtain Specific Consent to Past Board Decisions

Written minutes approval forms can be sent out to directors along with the prior minutes before the meeting to obtain signed approval of those minutes. Using this form can save time and has the added advantage of providing signed consent to previous decisions reached at meetings. This may be helpful, for example, if directors did not attend the last meeting and you wish to have a record of their approval to important decisions reached at that meeting. (How to prepare Approval of Corporate Minutes forms is covered in Chapter 7, Section B, Step 3.)

If you use an Approval of Corporate Minutes form to obtain written approval of minutes of a prior meeting, change this paragraph in the current minutes to read as follows:

The secretary announced that the minutes of the __[regular, annual or special directors]__ meeting held on __[date]__ , 19__, had been distributed prior to the meeting" and that each director had returned to the secretary of the corporation a signed statement showing approval of the minutes of the prior meeting. [Delete the next sentence in the form showing a vote was taken at the meeting.]

❾ If written or oral annual reports are presented to directors by officers, staff, outside accountants, lawyers or others, specify the nature of each report and the name of each presenter. We recommend that you use the following language to at least show annual reports by the corporate president and treasurer: "an annual financial report by the treasurer and an annual operations report by the president."

You may also want to show standing or ad hoc committee reports presented or distributed at the meeting.

Example: "report by the chairperson of the corporation's standing New Building Committee; report by the secretary of the Insurance Committee on the availability and cost of general liability and directors' and officers' errors and omissions insurance coverage"

❿ A standard item of business at an annual meeting of the board is the reappointment of the officers of the corporation and members of standing committees of the board. For small corporations, the president, vice president, secretary and treasurer are normally reappointed for another term, and all current standing committee members are also redelegated to their committees. However, this is a good time to make changes if officers, committee members or board members think it makes sense to do so.

Most smaller corporations do not set up separate committees of the board, since the board is small to start with. Instead, the board sets up one or more non-director committees comprised of officers, department managers and staff to tend particular aspects of corporate activity.

Example: Hare and Tortoise, Inc., a small publishing company, appoints a workers' benefits committee to meet throughout the year to discuss suggestions for improvements to workers' health and pension coverage. The board has also set up a building improvement committee that negotiates with the landlord for improvements to corporate headquarters. At the annual directors meeting, the board reestablishes the authority for each committee for another year and fills any vacancies and makes any replacements requested by each committee.

⓫ Another standard item of business at annual directors meetings is the award of annual salary increases, bonuses or additional fringe benefits to employees for work performance or results achieved during the preceding fiscal year. Use this paragraph for this purpose if you wish; leave it blank or delete it if it doesn't apply.

Either specify the name of each employee separately or specify groups or categories of employees, if you'd prefer. In the blanks at the right of the name of each employee (or group of employees), specify the amount and type of compensation or benefit approved by the directors.

Example: The Middle Road Management Corporation decides to award three of its VPs an additional bonus for their outstanding work performance during the preceding year. The corporation also rewards its entire customer service department for excellent work:

Name	Type and Amount of Compensation or Benefit
Mark Fuller	*$5,000 annual bonus*
Tricia Mueller	*$5,000 annual bonus*
Benjamin Bailey	*$5,000 annual bonus*
Customer Service	*10% annual bonus*

⓬ It's common to take action at annual directors meetings on extraordinary items not built into the minutes form. This section of the annual minutes allows you to document these additional decisions by inserting one or more resolutions in the space following this paragraph.

In the first blank, show the vote required for passage of the resolution, normally a majority of directors present at the meeting. See Chapter 4, Step 13a.) Then include the language of the resolution passed by the board.

In the space below the paragraph, insert one or more resolutions that describe the specific legal, tax, financial or other items of business voted upon and approved at the meeting. You don't need to use fancy or legal language for your resolution; just describe as specifically as you can the transaction or matter approved by your board in a short, concise statement. Normally, resolutions start with a preamble of the following sort: "The board or shareholders resolved that…" but this is not required.

Following are some examples.

Example 1 (Bank Loan): "The board resolved that the treasurer be authorized to obtain a loan from (name of bank) for the amount of $_____ on terms he/she considers commercially reasonable."

Example 2 (Corporate Hiring): "The board approved the hiring of (name of new employee), hired in the position of (job title) at an annual salary of $_____ and in accordance with the terms of the corporation's standard employment contract."

Example 3 (Tax Year): "The board decided that the corporation shall adopt a tax year with an ending date of 3/31."

Example 4 (Amendment of Articles): "The board of directors resolved that the following new article be added to the corporation's Articles of Incorporation (language of new article)."

If you have trouble finding or drafting a resolution, or if the matter has important legal or tax consequences, you may wish to turn to a lawyer or accountant for help. (See Chapter 9.)

Nolo's *Taking Care of Your Corporation, Vol. 2: Key Corporate Decisions Made Easy,* by Anthony Mancuso, contains ready-to-use resolutions for common corporate legal, tax, financial and business transactions. Also included in the tear-out and computer disk forms are backup forms, such as promissory notes, employment contracts and legal and tax information to help you take care of the business being approved by your board.

❸ This adjournment paragraph and concluding signature line should appear at the very end of your minutes after any specialized resolutions adopted by your board. Fill in the name of the secretary of the meeting under the signature line.

After obtaining the signature of the secretary, file the completed minutes in your corporate records book, together with all attachments. If you prepared a separate meeting folder to include material having to do with your meeting (such as reports, notice forms, and the like—see Chapter 3, Section B, Step 1), now is the time to transfer this material, along with your completed minutes, to your permanent corporate records book. This paperwork can come in handy later to show that your meeting was called, noticed and held properly. With respect to reports, the minutes will serve as a reminder of the reasons for decisions reached at your meeting.

C. Preparing Minutes for Special Directors Meetings

Unlike regular or annual meetings of directors scheduled in advance in your Bylaws, special directors meetings are called during the year to discuss and vote upon important items of corporate business.

Typical resolutions presented and approved at special meetings of the board are usually legal or tax-related decisions, such as:

- approval of a lease or real estate purchase agreement

- approval of a bank loan or line of credit

- approval of a standard employment or independent contractor hiring policy to be used by the corporation

- approval of an amendment to Articles or Bylaws, or

- authorization of the issuance of shares to new or existing shareholders.

Following is the minutes form to use to document the actions taken at a special meeting of your directors. This form is similar to the annual directors meeting form presented in Section B, just above, but it does not contain the annual agenda items included in the preceding form. Fill out the minutes that are contained on the corporate records disk and in Appendix C as you follow the sample form and special instructions below.

The filename for this form is DIRSPCL, followed by a three-letter filename extension according to the version of the file. For example, Word users should select and use the DIRSPCL.DOC file. (See Chapter 10 for information on selecting and using the computer disk files.)

MINUTES OF SPECIAL MEETING OF DIRECTORS OF

_____ [name of corporation] _____

An special meeting of the directors of the corporation was held on
_____, 19___ at ___:___ __.M., at ❶
_____ [location of meeting] _____, state of
_____, for the purpose(s) of ❷
_____
_____
_____.

_____ acted as chairperson, and
_____ acted as secretary of the meeting. ❸

The chairperson called the meeting to order.

The secretary announced that the meeting was called by
_____.❹

The secretary announced that the meeting was held pursuant to notice, if and as required under the Bylaws of this corporation, or that notice had been waived by all directors entitled to receive notice under the Bylaws. Copies of any certificates of mailing of notice prepared by the secretary of the corporation and any written waivers signed by directors entitled to receive notice of this meeting were attached to these minutes by the secretary. ❺

The secretary announced that the following directors were present at the meeting, representing a quorum of the board of directors: ❻

Name of Director

_____
_____
_____
_____
_____

The following persons were also present at the meeting: ❼

Name   Title

_____   _____

_____   _____

_____   _____

The secretary announced that the minutes of the ___["annual," "regular" or "special"___

___directors]___ meeting held on _____, 19___.

☐ had been distributed prior to

☐ were distributed at

☐ were read at

the meeting. After discussion, a vote was taken and the minutes of the meeting were approved by the directors in attendance. ❽

The following reports were presented at the meeting by the following persons: ❾

_____

_____.

The secretary announced that the next item of business was the consideration of one or more formal resolutions for approval by the board. After introduction and discussion, and upon motion duly made and carried by the affirmative vote of ___["a majority of" or other vote___

___requirement]___ directors in attendance at the meeting, the following resolutions were adopted by directors entitled to vote at the meeting: ❿

There being no further business to come before the meeting, it was adjourned on motion duly made and carried.

⓫

_____

_____, Secretary

Special Instructions

❶ Insert the date, time and place (street address, city and state) of the meeting. Director meetings usually are held at the principal office of the corporation, although most Bylaws allow meetings to be held anywhere.

❷ List the specific purpose(s) for which this special directors meeting was called. A similar statement of purpose(s) should have been included in your notice or waiver of notice form used for the meeting. (See Chapter 3, Section B, Step 5c, and Chapter 7, Section B, Step 1.)

❸ Insert the name and title of the persons who acted as chairperson and secretary of the meeting. Bylaws typically provide that the president or chairperson of the board presides at meetings of directors, and that the corporate secretary acts as meeting secretary.

Note. In the instructions for this form, we specify when we are referring to the secretary of the corporation. All other references are to the secretary of the meeting. Again, normally the secretary of the corporation and the secretary of the meeting will be one and the same.

❹ Indicate the person or persons who called the special meeting of directors, along with each person's title. Typically, Bylaws allow one of the directors, the president, or another corporate officer to call a special meeting of directors; see Chapter 3, Section B, Step 3a, and check your Bylaws.

❺ Proper notice or waiver of notice is important for special directors meetings. You want all directors to be fully informed of the time and purpose of all specially-called board meetings. We describe the legal requirements and practical procedure for preparing notice in Chapter 3, Section B, Step 5. Instead of providing notice, it's legal to have each director sign a written waiver of notice, as explained in Chapter 7, Section B, Step 1. Make sure to attach any written waivers of notice to your minutes. If you mailed actual notice to your directors before the meeting, you may wish to have your corporate secretary prepare and attach a Certificate of Mailing of notice as explained in Chapter 3, Section B, Step 9b.

❻ List the names of the directors present at the meeting. Normally, the Bylaws specify that a majority of the full number of directors represents a quorum for a directors meeting. Remember, if you don't have a quorum, you must adjourn the meeting. (See Chapter 4, Step 8a.)

❼ Specify any additional persons (other than the chairperson and secretary of the meeting) who attend the special board meeting but do not count towards a quorum. If reports are to be submitted to the directors, then additional corporate officers, staff or committee members may be in attendance, as well as the corporation's accountant or legal consultant.

❽ It is customary, though not legally necessary, for participants at a special meeting to approve the minutes of the previous directors meeting. Mostly this formality is undertaken to remind everyone of any special business approved at the last meeting and to allow any objections prior to placing a formal copy of the minutes in the corporate records book.

If you decide to follow this formality and wish to save time, you may send copies of the minutes of the last meeting to each participant to read prior to the meeting as explained in Chapter 7, Section B, Steps 3-5. Otherwise, distribute copies of the minutes or have the secretary read or summarize them. Then ask for voice approval. Normally, the minutes are routinely approved, but if there are objections, you will need to work them out before approving the minutes. You may make appropriate corrections to the minutes or obtain a majority vote to approve the minutes over the objection of one or more directors. Fill in the blanks as shown to indicate the method of distributing or announcing the minutes of the prior meeting to directors. If you choose not to address prior minutes at your meeting, either delete this entire paragraph or fill in "not applicable."

Use Written Approval Forms to Save Time or Obtain Specific Consent to Past Board Decisions

Written minutes approval forms can be sent out to directors along with the prior minutes before the meeting to obtain signed approval of those minutes. Using this form can save time and has the added advantage of providing signed consent to previous decisions reached at meetings. This may be helpful, for example, if directors did not attend the last meeting and you wish to have a record of their approval of important decisions reached at that meeting. (How to prepare Approval of Corporate Minutes forms is covered in Chapter 7, Section B, Step 3.)

If you use an Approval of Corporate Minutes form to obtain written approval of minutes of a prior meeting, change this paragraph in the current minutes to read as follows:

The secretary announced that the minutes of the   [regular, annual or special
directors]   meeting held on   [date] ,19 , had been distributed prior to the
meeting" and that each director had returned to the secretary of the corporation a
signed statement showing approval of the minutes of the prior meeting. [Delete the
next sentence in the form showing a vote was taken at the meeting.]

❾ If written or oral reports are presented to directors by officers, staff,
outside accountants, lawyers or others, specify the nature of each report and
the name and title of each presenter. For example, this might be: "a presentation by Tasha Browne, corporate vice president, on plans to expand the
company's current product line, and a report by the treasurer, Dan Woo, on
the amounts of additional bank loan funds that will be required to fund this
expansion."

❿ This section shows the main business of special directors meetings:
the consideration and approval of one or more formal resolutions. In the
first blank, show the vote required for passage of the resolution—normally
a majority of directors present at the meeting. (See Chapter 4, Step 13a.)
Then include the language of each resolution passed by the board in the
space shown.

Again, you don't need to use fancy or legal language for your resolution;
just describe as specifically as you can the transaction or matter approved
by your board in a short, concise statement. Normally, resolutions start
with a preamble of the following sort: "The board resolved that…" but this
is not required.

Following are some sample resolutions.

Example 1 (Bank Loan): " The board resolved that the treasurer be authorized
to obtain a loan from (name of bank) for the amount of $_____ on terms he/she
considers commercially reasonable."

Example 2 (Corporate Hiring): "The board approved the hiring of (name of
new employee), hired in the position of (job title) at an annual salary of $_____
and in accordance with the terms of the corporation's standard employment
contract."

Example 3 (Tax Year): "The board decided that the corporation shall adopt a
tax year with an ending date of 3/31."

Example 4 (Amendment of Articles): "*The board of directors resolved that the following new article be added to the corporation's Articles of Incorporation (language of new article).*"

If you have trouble finding or drafting a resolution, or if the matter has important legal or tax consequences, you may wish to turn to a lawyer or accountant for help (see Chapter 9).

Nolo's *Taking Care of Your Corporation, Vol. 2: Key Corporate Decisions Made Easy,* by Anthony Mancuso, contains ready-to-use resolutions for common corporate legal, tax, financial and business transactions. Also included in the tear-out and computer disk forms are backup forms, such as promissory notes, employment contracts, shareholder buy-sell provisions, and legal and tax information to help you take care of the business being approved by your board.

⓫ This concluding adjournment paragraph and signature line should appear at the very end of the minutes, after any resolutions. Fill in the name of the secretary of the meeting under the signature line.

After obtaining the signature of the secretary, file the printed minutes in your corporate records book, together with all attachments. If you prepared a separate meeting folder to include material having to do with your meeting (such as reports, notice forms and the like—see Chapter 3, Section B, Step 1), now is the time to transfer this material, along with your completed minutes, to your permanent corporate records book. This paperwork can come in handy later to show that your meeting was called, noticed and held properly. With respect to reports, the minutes will serve as a reminder of the reasons for decisions reached at your meeting.

CHAPTER 7

How to Hold a Paper Meeting of Your Directors or Shareholders

In this chapter, we present the few simple steps necessary to document a "paper" meeting of your directors or shareholders. With a paper meeting, shareholders or directors don't actually hold a meeting, but instead arrive at necessary decisions informally. To make a clear record of these decisions, minutes are prepared (normally by the president or secretary) and the directors or shareholders approve them by affixing their signatures.

A. Decide Whether to Hold a Paper Meeting

We've already touched upon the advantages and disadvantages of preparing minutes for a paper meeting in Chapter 2. Here we will make a few key points related to their use. The paper meeting procedure works best for corporations with only a few directors or shareholders who work together or know each other well and agree to most corporate decisions. Of course, paper meetings also work fine for a one-person corporation, where the sole shareholder-director really doesn't need to sit down and talk to himself (or if he does, then perhaps it's time for a two-week vacation).

In such small corporations, the paper meeting procedure allows corporate principals to elect officers and conduct other routine corporate business without going through the motions of holding a meeting. Legally, preparing and ratifying paperwork for a fictional corporate meeting will not present problems for your corporation as long as every shareholder or director agrees to the procedure and, of course, approves the decisions reflected in the minutes of the paper meeting.

Avoid Paper Meetings If There Is Conflict or Disagreement

Minutes of a paper meeting work best for small, closely-held corporations, with no more than a few shareholders and directors. However, even for small corporations, we suggest you only use this procedure for corporate decisions where everyone is really in agreement. If there is even a whiff of dissent in the wind, or if the decision requires additional discussion, it is far better to hold a real meeting.

1. Documenting Past Decisions With Paper Meetings

If you failed to properly document past annual and special meetings of your directors and shareholders, you are not alone. Many, if not most, smaller corporations that do their own paperwork forget to document important legal and tax decisions as they occur, putting off the task of preparing the paperwork until later. Often, the impetus for preparing this overlooked paperwork is an IRS audit or a request for minutes of a meeting from a bank or other financial institution.

As long as all directors and shareholders mutually agreed to the past actions when they were taken, using the paper meeting approach to recreate corporate records after the fact should work well for your corporation.

Example: Small Systems, Inc. is a small, closely-held corporation with six shareholder-directors who work in the business. They have been in operation for five years when they are notified of an IRS audit of their last two years' corporate income tax returns. For the audit, they need to produce corporate records for the years in question. Like many other small corporations, the daily grind of business has consumed the energies of each of the co-owners, and procedural niceties, such as annual meetings, have been skipped. Informally, and by mutual agreement, the initial directors named in the Articles of Incorporation have stayed on the board since the beginning of corporate existence, and the only special items of formal legal or tax paperwork executed during the first five years were the signing of a lease by the corporate president and treasurer, as well as the signing by the shareholders of an IRS S corporation tax election form.

The directors decide it is best to formalize these past decisions by preparing paper minutes for the annual directors and shareholders meeting for the last five years. They also decide to prepare minutes of a special directors meeting (approving the corporate lease) and a special shareholders meeting (approving the S corporation tax election). These minutes of paper meetings are placed in the corporate records book, and copies of the minutes of meetings for the two years in question are given to the IRS.

2. Comparison of Paper Meetings and Written Consents

As we have mentioned several times, for those who don't want to hold a formal directors or shareholders meeting, or missed holding one, there are two alternative procedures:

- preparing minutes of a paper meeting, or

- acting by written consent.

If you prepare minutes for a paper meeting, you are, in essence, approving corporate business by the unanimous written consent of your directors or shareholders, a procedure sanctioned by the corporate statutes of the various states. However, minutes of a paper meeting often look better in the corporate records and carry more weight, at least from a practical standpoint, than written consent forms.

Here is a recap of a few important points if you're still not sure whether paper meetings or written consents best meet your needs.

Use minutes of paper meetings for annual business. Minutes of paper meetings work best to show the discussion and approval of standard items of business taken up annually by the board or shareholders. Such business includes the annual review and discussion of past and present corporate business, the annual election of the directors, and acceptance by directors of another term on the board. The reason to use minutes of paper meetings for routine decisions is simple: the IRS, courts, financial institutions and others generally expect corporate records to contain standard minutes of meeting forms. Written consent forms with no supporting documentation just aren't enough normally to convince others that you paid attention to the ongoing formalities of corporate life.

Written consents may be used for special business. Written consent forms are generally adequate to document individual actions that would normally be approved at special meetings of your board or shareholders. These isolated decisions, approved during the year between annual directors or shareholders meetings, are commonly approved and documented with written consent forms rather than more formal minutes of a paper meeting.

Corporate records may contain minutes and consent forms. It's fine to prepare minutes of paper meetings for some decisions and written consents for others.

Example: Bertrand and Jackie are a married couple and the only two share-holder-directors of a small consulting business. They both work for the corporation and routinely re-elect themselves to the board each year. After a few years of operation, they realize that they haven't kept up their corporate records. Bertrand prepares minutes of annual shareholders meetings for the past two years showing the re-election of each director to the board. He accompanies these with minutes of annual directors meetings, showing the directors' acceptance of their re-election to the board each year. Of course, these minutes forms also show the discussion and approval of standard agenda items and business normally taken up at these meetings, such as reading and approval of past minutes and the approval of annual raises or bonuses to employees.

To save time and form preparation, Bertrand prepares written consent forms showing two special transactions—a change of corporate tax year recommended by the corporation's accountant and the approval of a ten-year lease for the corporate main office premises—approved by the directors between the dates of these annual meetings. Approval could also have been documented by preparing minutes of special meetings, but consent forms seem adequate, especially given the fact that the annual meetings are fully documented.

B. How to Prepare Minutes of Paper Meetings

If you've decided to hold a paper meeting, follow the steps below to prepare the necessary paperwork.

Step 1. Prepare a Waiver of Notice Form

If you're going to prepare minutes for a meeting that has not or will not occur, you'll obviously want to sidestep any formal call and notice requirements for holding the meeting. (See Chapter 3, Section B, Steps 3 and 5, for an overview of call and notice requirements contained in Bylaws and state corporate statutes.) The best way to do this from a legal perspective is to have each director or shareholder sign a written Waiver of Notice of Meeting form, dated before or on the same date of the meeting.

We strongly advise you to always summarize the purposes of the upcoming meeting in your Waiver of Notice of Meeting form. In some cases, it is legally required; we recommend it anyway to make sure all directors and shareholders appreciate the nature of the business to be taken up at the meeting.[1]

Other Reasons to Use a Waiver of Notice of Meeting Form

You may use a Waiver of Notice of Meeting form even if you're planning to hold a real meeting. As discussed earlier in Chapters 3 through 6, you should use a Waiver of Notice of Meeting form whenever you wish to hold a meeting of your board or shareholders and do not have or do not choose to take time to provide everyone with advance verbal or written notice.

---

[1] State laws usually prohibit the transaction of any business not specified in the Waiver of Notice for a special shareholders meeting.

WAIVERS OF NOTICE MAY BE USED FOR REAL MEETINGS

State corporate laws all allow waivers of notice for directors and shareholders meetings.

Directors meetings. All states specifically allow directors to sign a written waiver of any legal rights they have to prior notice of a meeting. The standard form used for this purpose is called in legal slang a "waiver of notice form." Typically, state laws also provide that even if a director didn't get proper formal notice of a meeting, but hears about it and attends, by the act of showing up, the director legally waives notice to any meeting unless he or she speaks up at the beginning of the meeting and objects to not having received proper notice of the meeting. In West Virginia, no notice of a directors meeting is required (notice is automatically waived) if all directors attend the meeting. (West Virginia Corporation Act § 31-1-72.)

Shareholders meetings. All states specifically allow shareholders to sign a written waiver of notice of meeting form, and, as with directors, most states provide that shareholders who attend a meeting without objection are assumed to have agreed to the notice or lack of notice for the meeting. Again, in West Virginia, no notice of a shareholders meeting is required if all shareholders attend the meeting in person or by proxy. (West Virginia Corporation Act § 31-1-72.)

Below is a sample of the Waiver of Notice of Meeting form included on the corporate records disk and in Appendix C. Fill it out as you follow the sample form with instructions below. By signing this form, the director or shareholder waives any notice requirements for the meeting otherwise required under state law and any additional or alternative notice rules set in your Bylaws.

You can prepare one Waiver of Notice of Meeting form for multiple directors or shareholders to sign, or you can prepare one form for each person.

The filename for this form is WAIVER, followed by a three-letter filename extension according to the version of the file. For example, Word users should select and use the WAIVER.DOC file. (See Chapter 10 for information on selecting and using the computer disk files.)

WAIVER OF NOTICE OF MEETING OF

_____ [name of corporation] _____

The undersigned __[name(s) of director(s) or shareholder(s)]__ waive(s) notice of and consent(s) to the holding of the __["annual," "regular" or "special"]__ meeting of the __["shareholders" or "directors"]__ of __[name of corporation]__ held at __[location of meeting]__, state of _____, on _____, 19___ at ___:___ __.M., for the purpose(s) of: ❶

_____

_____

_____.

Dated: _____ ❷

Signature   Printed Name

_____   _____

_____   _____

_____   _____

_____   _____

Special Instructions

❶ Under state corporate statutes, for certain important corporate decisions, such as the election of directors or amendment of Bylaws, a waiver of notice form is required to contain a description of the matter presented and approved at a meeting. When preparing a waiver of notice form, whether for a real or paper meeting, it's always important that you state the purpose of the meeting. Be as specific as you can regarding the proposals presented at the meeting.

Example: A meeting is held on paper to approve an amendment to increase the authorized voting shares of the corporation. The purpose of the meeting stated in the waiver reads as follows: "amending Article III of the Articles of Incorporation to increase the authorized voting shares of the corporation from 100,000 to 200,000 shares."

❷ If more than one person will sign the form, the date inserted here should be the date the first person signs the waiver form. This date should be on or before the meeting date.

Pass out All Paperwork at Once

In Steps 2 through 5, below, we recommend that you have directors or shareholders approve the minutes of a paper meeting. So, to avoid contacting directors or shareholders twice, prepare this extra paperwork first, then pass out all forms together.

Step 2. Prepare Minutes of the Paper Meeting

Your next step is to prepare the minutes for your paper meeting of directors or shareholders. Usually, the secretary of the corporation prepares and distributes this paperwork, but the task can be assigned to anyone.

To prepare minutes for an annual or special paper meeting of shareholders, follow the corresponding minutes form covered in Chapter 5. To prepare minutes for an annual or special paper meeting of directors, follow the appropriate form covered in Chapter 6.

Place your minutes of the paper meeting in your corporate records book, and make copies of the minutes for each director or shareholder to review prior to signing the Approval of Corporate Minutes form discussed in the next step.

Step 3. Prepare Approval of Corporate Minutes Form

After preparing minutes for your paper meeting, we recommend that you get each director or shareholder to specifically sign off on the decisions approved in the minutes. This step is essential when you use the paper meeting procedure to document past corporate decision-making; because a real meeting was not held, you need to be sure everyone agrees to your summary of the decisions reflected in your minutes.

Below is a sample of the Approval of Corporate Minutes form which is included on the enclosed corporate records disk and in Appendix C. Use this form to obtain approval of minutes of a paper meeting. You can prepare one Approval of Corporate Minutes form for multiple directors or share-holders to sign, or you can prepare one form for each person. Fill it out as you follow the sample form below.

When to Use an Approval Form for Minutes of Real Meetings

The Approval of Corporate Minutes form can come in handy to obtain approval of the past minutes of real meetings. For example, as we suggest in Chapters 5 and 6, prior to holding annual shareholders and directors meetings, you may wish to send the minutes of previous meetings to directors or shareholders to read before the meeting. Instead of waiting for the next meeting to approve these minutes, you may wish to ask them to sign an approval form—assuming, of course, they do not have corrections or additions to make. Doing this can save time at the meeting, as well as provide a signed document showing that the directors or shareholders specifically approved actions taken at a prior meeting. Especially if a director or shareholder missed a previous meeting, it's a good idea to make a written record of their signed approval to important decisions reached at that earlier meeting.

The filename for this form is APPROVE, followed by a three-letter filename extension according to the version of the file. For example, Word users should select and use the APPROVE.DOC file. (See Chapter 10 for information on selecting and using computer disk files.)

APPROVAL OF CORPORATE MINUTES OF

_____ [name of corporation] _____

The undersigned _["shareholder" or "directors"]_ consent(s) to the minutes of the _["annual," "regular" or "special"]_ meeting of the _["shareholders" or "directors"]_ of _[name of corporation]_ held at _[location of meeting]_ , state of _____, on _____, 19___ at ____:____ __.M., attached to this form, and accept(s) the resolutions passed and decisions made at such meeting as valid and binding acts of the _["shareholder" or "directors"]_ of the corporation.

Dated: _____ ❶

Signature   Printed Name

_____   _____

_____   _____

_____   _____

_____   _____

_____   _____

Special Instructions

❶ If this is an approval of minutes for a paper meeting, we suggest the approval be dated on or before the date set for the paper meeting.

Step 4. Prepare a Cover Letter

Below, we present a sample of the cover letter included on the corporate records disk and in Appendix C. You may wish to send along this letter with your approval form when mailing minutes out to directors or shareholders. This letter explains the reasons for asking for approval of paper minutes and can come in handy if your directors or shareholders are not corporate insiders or are unfamiliar with corporate procedures and formalities.

The filename for this form is PAPERLET, followed by a three-letter filename extension according to the version of the file. For example, Word users should select and use the PAPERLET.DOC file. (See Chapter 10 for information on selecting and using computer disk files.)

COVER LETTER FOR APPROVAL OF MINUTES OF PAPER MEETING

Date: _____

Name: _____

Mailing Address: _____

City, State, Zip: _____

Re: Approval of Minutes

Dear _____:

      I am enclosing minutes of a meeting of the ___["shareholders" or "directors"]___ of ___[name of corporation]___ that show approval of one or more specific resolutions. Each resolution contains the language of an item of business approved by the ___["shareholders" or "directors"]___ in the past.

      Since these items were agreeable to the ___["shareholders" or "directors"]___, we did not hold a formal meeting to approve these decisions. We are now finalizing our corporate records and preparing formal minutes that reflect prior corporate decisions.

      To confirm that these minutes accurately reflect the past decisions reached by the ___["shareholders" or "directors"]___, please date and sign the enclosed Approval of Corporate Minutes form and mail it to me at the address below. If you have corrections or additions to suggest, please contact me so we can hold a meeting or make other arrangements for formalizing and documenting these changes.

Sincerely,

___[signature]_____

Enclosures: Minutes & Approval of Corporate Minutes forms

Please return to:

Name: _____

Corporation: _____

Mailing Address: _____

City, State, Zip: _____

Phone: _____ Fax: _____

Step 5. Get Directors and Shareholders Approval

After you've completed the forms (Steps 1-4, above), make copies. Then distribute the forms to each director or shareholder. If it's easier, you may send around one copy of the forms to be signed; this is particularly efficient when shareholders or directors all work at the business.

Remember to include:

- Waiver of Notice of Meeting forms

- Minutes, along with any reports or attachments, and

- Approval of Corporate Minutes.

After you've completed your paperwork and obtained signed copies, place the signed documents in your corporate records book.

CHAPTER 8

How to Take Action by Written Consent Without a Meeting

Throughout previous chapters, we have pointed out that state statutes allow the directors and shareholders of a corporation to take action without holding a meeting simply by signing written consent forms. Basically, this consists of all the shareholders or directors signing a piece of paper that contains the language of the decision (resolution) to be approved.

Taking the written consent approach to corporate decision-making is often appropriate for small corporations with only a few shareholders or directors. It's sometimes even suitable for slightly larger organizations that don't have time to assemble the board of directors or shareholders at a special meeting and meet a deadline for making a decision.

Action by written consent is most appropriate if the issue at hand is a routine tax or financial formality, for instance the approval of standard loan terms offered by the corporation's bank or the approval of a tax election recommended by the corporation's accountant. It is not appropriate where a decision may engender debate or disagreement among directors or shareholders.

WHEN TO USE MINUTES OF PAPER MEETINGS INSTEAD OF WRITTEN CONSENTS

Even small corporations usually prepare minutes of a real or paper meeting to document the decisions made at annual directors and shareholders meetings. These take a little more time to prepare, but look more convincing and official in the corporate records book. (See Chapters 5 and 6 for instructions on preparing minutes of directors and shareholders meetings. Chapter 7 covers how to hold paper meetings.)

You can safely use written consents to show the approval of the type of individual decisions that would otherwise be documented by preparing minutes of a special directors or shareholders meeting.

In the steps below, we discuss the legal rules related to taking action by written consent. We provide a sample form with instructions that you can follow as you fill out the Written Consent to Action Without Meeting form included in Appendix C and on the corporate records disk. You'll see that it only takes a minute or two to fill out this form, which must then be distributed to your directors or shareholders for signing.

Provide Written Consents to Absent Directors or Shareholders

Written consent forms also come in handy when a director or shareholder is not able to attend an important corporate meeting. Even though you obtain a quorum and therefore legally approve decisions at a meeting, it's wise to get the written consent of any non-attending directors, especially where important resolutions are adopted. Doing this ensures that all directors or shareholders are informed of actions taken at the meeting, and it provides clear evidence of their assent to the action taken.

Step 1. Check Bylaws for Your State's Written Consent Rules

Start by checking your Bylaws to determine your corporation's rules for taking action by written consent. The most common requirement is that directors and shareholders can only take action without a meeting by the *unanimous* written consent of directors or shareholders. Some states do, however, allow fewer than all shareholders to approve decisions by written consent as explained below.

Don't get too caught up in the Bylaws' language on this issue. If you follow our practical suggestion to have all written consents signed by every director or shareholder, you should meet the statutory requirements for written consents in your state.

a. Director Written Consent Laws

All states have a corporate law statute authorizing director action by written consent (without a meeting). In every state except Tennessee, the written consent of *all* directors is required for the consent to be valid.[1] Therefore, if you learn, or suspect, that one or more directors may object, you need to hold a meeting to approve the matter at hand.

b. Shareholder Written Consent Rules

All states allow shareholder action by written consent. A majority of states require unanimous shareholder consent to the action—in other words, all shareholders entitled to vote on a matter must sign the consent form. About 20 states allow approval by less than the unanimous written consent of shareholders. In these states, a common rule is that shareholders owning or representing the number of shares required for passage of the action at a meeting at which all shareholders are present are required to sign the consent form.[2] In other words, in states that follow this special rule, a majority of all the outstanding voting shares of the corporation must sign the written consent form.

You may live in a state with other rules, such as one that allows less than unanimous written consent by shareholders in all matters except the election of directors, which must be approved by all shares. Again, check your Bylaws for the specific shareholder written consent rule in your state.

---

[1] In Tennessee, although all directors must consent to the process of approving an action by written consent, only the number of directors required for a vote at a meeting (a majority of the full board) need to signify their approval on the written consent form (the remaining directors should vote "no" or indicate their abstention on the written consent form). See Tennessee Business Corporation Act § 48-18-202.

[2] Arkansas, California, Delaware, Florida, Georgia, Illinois, New Jersey, Oklahoma and Wisconsin follow this special rule for most shareholder decisions, but may require unanimity for special shareholder actions such as an increase in the stock or indebtedness of the corporation. The remaining 11 states follow different practices— for example, Kentucky requires the written consent of 80% of the shares; Iowa requires 90%. As always, check your Bylaws for the shareholder written consent rules in your state.

Have All Directors or Shareholders Sign a Consent Form

We recommend that you always obtain the unanimous written consent of *all* directors or shareholders. Doing so not only ensures that you will meet the most stringent state law requirements for director or shareholder written consents, but gives notice to every director and shareholder of the decision. Regardless of the legal requirements, if you expect opposition by one or more directors or shareholders to a decision and can't achieve unanimity, it makes sense to hold a meeting to discuss these differences and obtain a vote on the issue instead.

Step 2. Prepare Written Consent Form

Below is a sample of the Written Consent to Action Without Meeting form included on the enclosed corporate records disk and in Appendix C. Fill it out as you follow the sample form with instructions below.

The filename for this form is CONSENT, followed by a three-letter filename extension according to the version of the file. For example, Word users should select and use the CONSENT.DOC file. (See Chapter 10 for information on selecting and using computer disk files.)

WRITTEN CONSENT TO ACTION WITHOUT MEETING

The undersigned   ["shareholders" or directors"]   ❶ of   [name of corporation]

hereby consent(s) as follows: ❷

_____

_____

_____

_____

_____

_____

_____

_____

_____

_____.

Dated: _____ ❸

Signature   Printed Name

_____   _____

_____   _____

_____   _____

_____   _____

_____   _____

Special Instructions

❶ Indicate whether you are preparing this consent form to show action taken without a meeting by either your directors or shareholders. If you want both the directors and shareholders to approve a given action, prepare separate forms.

❷ Insert a description of the actions or decisions agreed to by the directors or shareholders in the form of a resolution. You don't need to use fancy or legal language for your resolution; just describe as specifically as you can the transaction or matter approved by your board or shareholders in a short, concise statement. Normally, resolutions start with a preamble of the following sort: "The (board or shareholders) resolves that…" but this is not required.

Following are some sample resolutions.

Example 1 (Bank Loan): "The board resolved that the treasurer be authorized to obtain a loan from (name of bank) for the amount of $_____ on terms he/she considers commercially reasonable."

Example 2 (Corporate Hiring): "The board approved the hiring of (name of new employee), hired in the position of (job title) at an annual salary of $_____ and in accordance with the terms of the corporation's standard employment contract."

Example 3 (Tax Year): "The board decided that the corporation shall adopt a tax year with an ending date of 3/31."

Example 4 (Amendment of Articles): "The shareholders resolved that the following new article be added to the corporation's Articles of Incorporation: (language of new article)."

If you have trouble finding or drafting a resolution, or if the matter has important legal or tax consequences, you may wish to turn to a lawyer or accountant for help (see Chapter 9).

Nolo's *Taking Care of Your Corporation, Vol. 2: Key Corporate Decisions Made Easy,* by Anthony Mancuso, contains ready-to-use resolutions for common corporate legal, tax, financial and business transactions. Also included in the tear-out and computer disk forms are back-up forms, such as promissory notes, employment contracts, shareholder buy-sell provisions, and legal and tax information to help you take care of the business being approved by your board or shareholders.

❸ Date the consent form and have your directors or shareholders sign their names. If you have only a few directors or shareholders, it may be easiest to prepare one master consent form to be relayed to each of your directors or shareholders to sign. In this case, date the form as of the date of the first signature by a director or shareholder. Another method, more appropriate when you have a larger number of directors or shareholders, is to prepare a separate consent form for dating and signing by each director or shareholder. Either method works.

Reminder

We recommend that you have all directors or all shareholders sign the consent form. However, if your Bylaws allow your shareholders to take the action at hand by less than unanimous written consent, you can have a lesser number of the group sign the form if you are comfortable doing so.

Step 3. Place Signed Consent Forms in Your Corporate Records Book

After distributing your Written Consent to Action Without Meeting forms and obtaining the signatures of your directors or shareholders, make sure to place each completed form in your corporate records book. It's common to place these papers in the minutes section of the corporate records book, arranged according to the date of the action by written consent.

C HAPTER 9

Lawyers, Tax Specialists and Legal Research

Much of the work in holding corporate meetings and documenting decisions is routine. Any knowledgeable and motivated businessperson can competently do the work himself or herself. But there's no way around it—from time to time you are bound to need help from outside sources. Some corporate decisions involve complex areas of law or taxation. Others involve a mix of business and legal savvy and are likely to be best made with the input of an experienced small business lawyer.

As we have discussed earlier, you may wish to turn to a lawyer for help in drafting resolutions to approve special items of business approved at meetings or with written consents of your directors and shareholders. And, of course, there will be important legal consequences associated with ongoing corporate decisions that may require input from an experienced legal professional. Obviously, one good way to learn more about any legal decision or form is to read up on these areas in a law or business library. (See Section C, below.) Or you can decide, as many busy business people do, to pay a lawyer, accountant or financial advisor (such as a pension plan specialist, bank loan officer or financial investment advisor) to check your conclusions about tricky legal areas and the completion of legal formsl. In the sections below, we provide a few tips to help you in your search for competent expert information, assistance and advice.

A. How to Find the Right Lawyer

Most small businesses can't afford to put a lawyer on retainer. Even when consulted on an issue-by-issue basis, lawyer's fees mount up fast—way too fast in most instances for legal advice to be affordable except for the most pressing problems. Just as with individuals, more and more small businesses are trying to at least partially close this legal affordability gap by doing as much of their own legal form preparation as possible. Often a knowledgeable self-helper can sensibly accomplish the whole task. Other times, it makes sense to briefly consult with a lawyer at an interim stage, or have the paperwork reviewed upon completion.

You already have taken one positive step in the direction of making your legal life affordable by deciding to use the forms in this book to prepare standard corporate minutes and written consent forms. Depending on the size of your business and the complexity of your legal needs, your next step is likely to be to find a cooperative lawyer who will help you draft resolutions to approve complex or important legal decisions, such as the approval of stock buy-back provisions, employment contracts, or pension plan and fringe benefit packages.[1]

You obviously don't want a lawyer who is programmed to try and take over all your legal decision-making and form-drafting while running up billable hours as fast as possible. Instead, you need what we call a *legal coach*, someone who is willing to work with you—not just *for* you. Under this model, the lawyer works to help you take care of many routine legal matters yourself, also being available to consult on more complicated legal issues as the need arises. Over time, your legal coach makes a decent, but not extravagant, living helping you—and others—help themselves.

You Don't Need a Big-time Corporate Lawyer

There is a big lawyer surplus these days, and many newer lawyers, especially, are open to non-traditional business arrangements. Look for a lawyer with some small business experience, preferably in your field or area of operations. For the most part, you don't want a lawyer who works with big corporations. Not only will this person deal with issues that are far from your concerns, but he or she is almost sure to charge too much.

---

[1]As noted later in this chapter, ready-made resolutions to handle ongoing legal decisions of this sort are contained in Nolo's *Taking Care of Your Corporation, Vol. 2: Key Corporate Decisions Made Easy*, by Anthony Mancuso.

> **DON'T ASK A LAWYER FOR TAX ADVICE**
>
> When it comes to corporate decisions that have tax implications, such as the type and number of shares to issue, the best share buy-sell provisions to adopt, or the most advantageous employee benefit plan to consider, accountants often have a better grasp of the issues than lawyers. And an added bonus is that although tax advice doesn't come cheap, accountants often charge less than lawyers.

1. Look and Ask Around

When you go looking for a lawyer, don't start with phone books, legal directories or advertisements. Lawyer referral services operated by bar associations are equally unhelpful. These simply supply the names of lawyers who have signed onto the service, often accepting the lawyer's own word for what types of skills he or she has. A better approach is to talk to people in your community who own or operate businesses you respect. Ask them about their lawyer and what they think of that person's work. If you talk to half a dozen business people, chances are you'll come away with several good leads. Other people, such as your banker, accountant, insurance agent or real estate broker may be able to provide the names of lawyers they trust to help them with business matters. Friends, relatives and business associates within your own company may also have names of possible lawyers.

Let Your Legal Coach Refer You to Experts When Necessary

What if you have a very technical legal question? Should you start by seeking out a legal specialist? For starters, the answer is probably no. First, find a good business lawyer to act as your coach. Then rely on this person to suggest specialized materials or experts as the need arises.

2. Talk to the Lawyer Ahead of Time

After you get the names of several good prospects, don't wait until a legal problem arises before contacting a lawyer. Once enmeshed in a crisis, you may not have time to find a lawyer who will work with you at affordable rates. Chances are you'll wind up settling for the first person available at a moment's notice—almost a guarantee you'll pay too much for poor service.

When you call a lawyer, announce your intentions in advance—that you are looking for someone who is willing to review your papers from time to time, point you in the right direction as the need arises, serve as a legal advisor as circumstances dictate, and tackle particular legal problems if necessary. In exchange for this, let the lawyer know you are willing to pay promptly and fairly. If the lawyer seems agreeable to this arrangement, ask to come in to meet for a half hour or so. Although many lawyers will not charge you for this introductory appointment, it's often a good idea to offer to pay for it. You want to establish that while you are looking for someone to help you help yourself, you are not looking for a free ride.

At the interview, re-emphasize that you are looking for a non-traditional "legal coach" relationship. Many lawyers will find this unappealing—for example, saying they don't feel comfortable reviewing documents you have drafted using self-help materials. If so, thank the person for being frank and keep interviewing other lawyers. You'll also want to discuss other important issues in this initial interview, such as the lawyer's customary charges for services, as explained further below.

Pay particular attention to the rapport between you and your lawyer. Remember—you are looking for a legal coach who will work with you. Trust your instincts and seek a lawyer whose personality and business sense are compatible with your own.

3. Set the Extent and Cost of Services in Advance

When you hire a lawyer, get a clear understanding about how fees will be computed. For example, if you call the lawyer from time-to-time for general advice or to be steered to a good information source, how will you be billed? Some lawyers bill a flat amount for a call or a conference; others bill to the nearest six-, ten- or twenty-minute interval. Whatever the lawyer's system, you need to understand it.

Especially at the beginning of your relationship, when you bring a big job to a lawyer, ask specifically about what it will cost. If you feel it's too much, don't hesitate to negotiate; perhaps you can do some of the routine work yourself, thus reducing the fee.

It's a good idea to get all fee arrangements—especially those for good-sized jobs—in writing. In several states, fee agreements between lawyers and clients must be in writing if the expected fee is $1,000 or more, or is contingent on the outcome of a lawsuit. But whether required or not, it's a good idea to get it in writing.

Use Non-lawyer Professionals to Cut Down on Legal Costs

Often, non-lawyer professionals perform some tasks better and at less cost than lawyers. For example, look to management consultants for strategic business planning, real estate brokers or appraisers for valuation of properties, brokerage houses for small public or private placements of shares, financial planners for investment advice, accountants for preparation of financial proposals, insurance agents for advice on insurance protection, independent paralegals for routine corporate resolution or form-drafting and CPAs for the preparation of tax returns. Each of these matters is likely to have a legal aspect, and you may eventually want to consult your lawyer, but normally you won't need to until you've gathered information on your own.

HOW LAWYERS CHARGE FOR LEGAL SERVICES

There are no across-the-board arrangements on how lawyers' fees are to be charged. Expect to be charged by one of the following methods:

- *By the hour.* In most parts of the United States, you can get competent services for your small business for $150 to $250 an hour. Newer attorneys still in the process of building a practice may be available for paperwork review, legal research and other types of legal work at lower rates.

- *Flat fee for a specific job.* Under this arrangement, you pay the agreed-upon amount for a given project, regardless of how much or how little time the lawyer spends. Particularly when you first begin working with a lawyer and are worried about hourly costs getting out of control, negotiating a flat fee for a specific job can make sense. For example, the lawyer may draw a real estate purchase agreement for $300, or review and finalize your share buy-sell provisions for $500.

- *Contingent fee based upon settlement amounts or winnings.* This type of fee typically occurs in personal injury, products liability, fraud and discrimination type cases, where a lawsuit will likely be filed. The lawyer gets a percentage of the recovery (often 33%-40%) if you win and nothing if you lose. Since most small business legal needs involve advice and help with drafting paperwork, a contingency fee approach doesn't normally make sense. However, if your business becomes involved in a personal injury claim or lawsuit involving fraud, unfair competition or the infringement of a patent or copyright, you may want to explore the possibility of a contingency fee approach.

- *Retainer.* Some corporations can afford to pay relatively modest amounts, perhaps $1,000 to $2,000 a year, to keep a business lawyer on retainer for ongoing phone or in-person consultations or routine business matters during the year. Of course, your retainer won't cover a full-blown legal crisis, but it may help take care of routine contract and other legal paperwork preparation and review during the year.

4. Confront Any Problems Head-On

If you have any questions about a lawyer's bill or the quality of his or her services, speak up. Buying legal help should be just like purchasing any other consumer service—if you are dissatisfied, seek a reduction in your bill or make it clear that the work needs to be redone properly (a better buy-sell agreement, a more comprehensive lease, etc.). If the lawyer runs a decent business, he or she will promptly and positively deal with your concerns. If you don't get an acceptable response, find another lawyer pronto. If you switch lawyers, you are entitled to get your important documents back from the first lawyer.

Even if you fire your lawyer, you may still feel unjustly wronged. If you can't get satisfaction from the lawyer, write to the client grievance office of your state bar association (with a copy to the lawyer, of course). Often, a phone call from this office to your lawyer will bring the desired results.

B. Finding the Right Tax Advisor

Many corporate resolutions and ongoing corporate decisions involve tax issues and advice (such as selecting a corporate tax year, approving tax-deductible fringe benefits or charging a reasonable rate of interest on corporate loans).[2] To make good decisions in these and other complicated areas may require the expert advice of a tax advisor. Depending on the issue before you, this advisor may be a certified public accountant, financial or investment advisor, corporate loan officer at a bank, pension plan specialist, or an inside or outside bookkeeper trained in employment and corporate tax reporting and return requirements.

Whatever your arrangement, consider the same issues for finding, choosing, using and resolving problems with a tax professional as those discussed in Section A, above, for legal services. Shop around for someone recommended by small business people you respect, or who is otherwise known to you as qualified for the task. Again, you may be able to take advantage of the lower rates offered by newer local practitioners or firms. Your tax person should be available over the phone to answer routine questions, or by mail or fax to handle paperwork and correspondence, with a minimum of formality or ritual. It is likely that you will spend much more time dealing with your tax advisor than your legal advisor, so be particularly attentive to the personal side of this relationship.

---

[2]Again, resolutions and background information to help you with these and other ongoing corporate tax decisions are contained in Nolo's *Taking Care of Your Corporation, Vol. 2: Key Corporate Decisions Made Easy*, by Anthony Mancuso.

Tax issues are often cloudy and subject to a range of interpretations and strategies, so it is absolutely essential that you discuss and agree to the level of tax-aggressiveness you expect from your advisor. Some small business owners want to live on the edge, saving every possible tax dollar, even at the risk that deductions and other tax practices will be frequently challenged by the IRS or state tax agents. Others are willing to pay a bit more in taxes to gain an extra measure of peace of mind. Whatever your tax strategy, make sure you find a tax advisor who feels the same way you do, or is willing to defer to your more liberal or conservative tax tendencies.

As with legal issues that affect your business, it pays to learn as much as you can about corporate and employment taxation. Not only will you have to buy less help from professionals, but you'll be in a good position to make good financial and tax planning decisions. IRS forms, business and law library publications, trade groups and countless other sources provide accessible information on corporate tax issues. Your accountant or other tax advisor should be able to help you put your hands on good materials. Banks are an excellent source of financial advice, particularly if they will be corporate creditors—after all, they will have a stake in the success of your corporation. Further, the federal Small Business Administration can prove to be an ideal source of financial and tax information and resources (as well as financing in some cases).

Resources for Tax and Financial Information

Following are just a few suggestions for finding additional tax and financial information relevant to running your corporation. If you want free copies of IRS publications, you can pick them up at your local IRS office or order by phone; call the toll-free IRS forms and publications request telephone number 1-800-TAX-FORM.

- Start by obtaining IRS Publication 509, *Tax Calendars*, prior to the beginning of each year. This pamphlet contains tax calendars showing the dates for corporate and employer filings during the year.

- You can find further information on withholding, depositing, reporting and paying federal employment taxes in IRS Publication 15, Circular E, *Employer's Tax Guide*, and the Publication 15 Supplement, as well as IRS Publication 937, *Business Reporting*. Also helpful are IRS Publication 542, *Tax Information on Corporations,* and IRS Publication 334, *Tax Guide for Small Business.*

- You'll find helpful information on accounting methods and bookkeeping procedures in IRS Publication 538, *Accounting Periods and Methods*, and IRS Publication 583, *Information for Business Taxpayers.*

- Other helpful sources of tax information include *Small-Time Operator,* by Kamaroff (Bell Springs Publishing, available through Nolo Press), an excellent primer on business bookkeeping practices that contains ledgers and worksheets, as well as *Starting Your Business*, by Crouch (Allyear Tax Guides), an investor and business tax guide.

C. How to Do Your Own Legal Research

Law is information, not magic. If you can look up necessary information yourself, you need not purchase it from a lawyer—although if it involves important issues, you may wish to check your conclusions with a lawyer, or use one as a sounding board for your intended course of action.

Much of the research necessary to understand your state's business corporation law can be done without a lawyer by spending a few minutes in a local law or business library. We explain the few simple steps necessary to find corporate statutes in your state's business corporation law in Chapter

1, Section D. Even if you need to go to a lawyer for help in preparing a corporate resolution to insert in your corporate minutes or to discuss the legal ramifications of a proposed corporate transaction, you can give yourself a leg up on understanding the legal issues surrounding your paperwork by reading practice manuals prepared for lawyers and law students at law and business libraries.

How do you find a law library open to the public? In many states, you need to look only as far as your county courthouse or, failing that, your state capitol. In addition, publicly funded law schools generally permit the public to use their libraries, and some private law schools grant limited access to their libraries—sometimes for a modest user's fee. If you're lucky enough to have access to several law libraries, select one that has a reference librarian to assist you. Also look through the business or reference department of a major city or county public library. These often carry corporate statutes as well as books on corporate law and taxation useful to the small business owner.

In doing legal research for a corporation or other type of business, there are a number of sources for legal rules, procedures and issues that you may wish to examine. Here are a few:

- *Business Corporation Act (BCA)*. These state statutes should be your primary focus for finding the rules for operating your corporation, including holding meetings and obtaining the approval of directors and shareholders to ongoing legal, tax, business and financial decisions. (See Chapter 1, Section D, for information on researching your state's BCA. A state-by-state listing of the names of state statutes is contained in Appendix B.)

- *Other state laws, such as the Securities, Commercial, Civil, Labor and Revenue Code*. These and other laws govern the issuance and transfer of corporate shares; the content, approval and enforcement of commercial contracts; employment practices and procedures; corporate and employment tax requirements; and other aspects of doing business in your state. Depending on the type of business you have, you may also want to research statutes and regulations dealing with other legal topics such as environmental law, product liability, real estate, copyrights and so on.

- *Federal laws*. These include the tax laws and procedures found in the Internal Revenue Code and Treasury Regulations implementing these code sections; regulations dealing with advertising, warranties and other consumer matters adopted by the Federal Trade Commission; and equal opportunity statutes such as Title VII of the Civil Rights Act administered by the Justice Department and Equal Employment Opportunities Commission.

- *Administrative rules and regulations.* Issued by federal and state administrative agencies charged with implementing statutes, state and federal statutes are often supplemented with regulations that clarify the statute and contain rules for an agency to follow in implementing and enforcing the statute. For example, most states have enacted special administrative regulations under their securities statutes that provide exemptions to stock issuance registration for small corporations and contain rules for corporations to follow and forms to file to rely on these exemptions. These rules allow corporations with a limited number of shareholders to issues shares without going to the time and expense of obtaining a permit to issue shares from their state's Securities Board.

- *Case law.* These are decisions of federal and state courts interpreting statutes—and sometimes making law, known as "common law," if the subject isn't covered by a statute. As we mention in Chapter 1, Section D, annotated state corporation codes contain not only the statute itself, but invaluable references to court cases interpreting and implementing specific provisions of the state's business corporation law.

- *Secondary sources.* Also important in researching corporate and business law are sources that provide background information on particular areas of law. One example is this book. Others are commonly found in the business, legal or reference section of your local bookstore.

Consider Joining a Trade Group

As a final recommendation to finding your own legal information, we suggest joining and participating in one or more trade groups related to your business. These groups often track legislation in particular areas of business and provide sample contracts and other useful legal forms. Some also retain law firms for trade association purposes that may be able to refer you to competent local lawyers.

RESOURCES FROM NOLO PRESS

Below are a few titles published by Nolo Press that we believe offer valuable information to the small business person:

- *Taking Care of Your Corporation, Vol. 2: Key Corporate Decisions Made Easy*, by Anthony Mancuso. This second book in the series contains corporate resolutions that can be included in corporate minutes or written consent forms to show approval of specific items of corporate legal and tax business. For example, the book shows how to document the adoption of a pension or profit-sharing plan, authorize the purchase or lease of real estate, and approve stock buy-sell restrictions. This book provides a brief discussion of important legal and tax considerations and rules associated with the various items of business reflected in these resolutions, as well as backup forms that help you take care of corporate business—corporate promissory notes to back up the approval of a loan, employment agreements to back up the hiring of a key corporate employee, and the like.

- *Legal Guide to Starting and Running a Small Business,* by Fred S. Steingold. This book is an essential resource for every small business owner, whether you are just starting out or are already established. Find out how to form a sole proprietorship, partnership or corporation, negotiate a favorable lease, hire and fire employees, write contracts and resolve business disputes.

- *The Employer's Legal Handbook,* by Fred S. Steingold. Employers need legal advice daily. Here's a comprehensive resource they can refer to over and over again for questions about hiring, firing and everything in between. The only book that compiles all the basics of employment law in one place, it covers: safe hiring practices, wages, hours, tips and commission, employee benefits, taxes and liability, insurance, discrimination, sexual harassment and termination.

- *Tax Savvy for Small Business*, by Frederick W. Daily. Gives business owners information they need about federal taxes and shows them how to make the best tax decisions for their business, maximize their profits and stay out of trouble with the IRS.

- How to Write a Business Plan, by Mike McKeever. If you're thinking of starting a business or raising money to expand an existing one, this book will show you how to write the business plan and loan package necessary to finance your business and make it work. Includes up-to-date sources of financing.

- *Patent It Yourself,* by David Pressman. This state-of-the art guide is a must for any inventor who wants to get a patent—from the patent search to the actual application. Patent attorney and former patent examiner David Pressman covers use and licensing, successful marketing and infringement. This best-selling book is now available in software as well. (System requirements: 4 MB RAM, Windows 3.1 or higher. VGA or higher monitor. Mouse and hard disk required.)

- *The Copyright Handbook: How to Protect and Use Written Works,* by Stephen Fishman. Provides forms and step-by-step instructions for protecting all types of written expression under U.S. and international copyright law. It also explains copyright infringement, fair use, works for hire and transfers of copyright ownership.

- *Software Development: A Legal Guide* (Book with disk: dual PC/Mac format), by Stephen Fishman. A reference bible for people in the software industry, this book with disk explores the legal ins and outs of copyright, trade secrets and patent protection, employment agreements, working with independent contractors and employees, development and publishing agreements and multimedia developments. Sample agreements and contracts are included on disk.

Computer User's Guide

This chapter contains background information on and step-by-step instructions for using the forms on the computer disk that accompanies this book. For brevity, we refer to this disk as the "corporate records disk" or the "computer disk."

Users with even a small degree of familiarity with their computer and word processing program should find the process of using the forms on the computer disk simple and straightforward. Please note, however, that the instructions below are meant primarily as reminders and tips on performing basic computer and word processor operations—not as a comprehensive tutorial. An understanding of basic computer operations such as booting up, copying disks and files, and running your word processing program is essential in following the material below. This is particularly important for PC users who need to understand correct DOS command line syntax and usage, how to log on to different disks (and, if using a hard disk, make and change directories), special key combinations used by PC word processing programs to perform basic operations, etc. So, if these tasks are new to you, please read your computer and word processor manuals before following the steps below.

See the README.TXT File on the Disk

For information on the latest updates and a summary of the files contained on the enclosed computer disk, see the README.TXT file contained on the disk. To do this, insert the corporate records disk in your A: drive, then use the **TYPE: A:README.TXT** or **MORE < A:README.TXT** command at the DOS prompt to view this file on the screen.

Important: Each word processor uses different commands to open, format, save and print documents. Nolo's technical support staff can help you if you have a particular problem with the corporate records disk, but they will refer you to your word processor manual if you are unfamiliar with the commands necessary to perform these operations. Please read your word processor manual for specific instructions on performing these tasks if you need additional help after reading the general instructions in this chapter.

Be Careful When Changing the Forms

We advise against making substantive changes to the forms on the disk. If you wish to add special provisions to the forms, make sure your changes conform to law—check your work against the relevant legal provisions or have your revised forms checked by a lawyer. (See Chapter 9.)

A. Contents of the Disk

This book includes a disk containing the corporate records forms discussed in preceding chapters of this book. Sample forms and specific instructions for filling in the blanks on each computer form are contained in the chapter that covers each form.

1. Disk Formats

The disk included with this package is provided in PC/MS-DOS format. This 3½" disk is formatted as a double-sided, double-density disk and holds 720 kilobytes. This format is appropriate for current PC/MS-DOS or older systems that have a 3½" disk drive.

Macintosh users. While the files are distributed on a PC/MS-DOS disk, most of the newer Macintosh computers (those with a 3½" SuperDrive such as the SE 30, Classic, II si, II cx, II ci or PowerBook) can read this disk. Macintosh users with a SuperDrive also need a DOS disk mounting program (usually a control panel file that must be placed in the System folder) such as PC Exchange or DOS Mounter. The files on the PC disk can be opened directly by a corresponding Macintosh program (for example, the Word for DOS files can be opened by Word for the Macintosh) or the text-only files can be imported to any Mac word processor. In the latter case, the extra line feeds that appear at the end of each DOS text file paragraph need to be deleted. The Apple File Exchange program can make this conversion for you; see your Apple documentation for instructions on doing this.

2. Types of Files

There are three sets of files on the corporate records disk, each of which contains a copy of each file saved in a separate file format. It's easy to spot the different formats: Each filename ends with a two- or three-letter filename extension signifying the format of the file, as follows:

- .DOC at the end of a filename means the file is a Microsoft Word for DOS version 5.0 file. This format is also readable by the Microsoft Word for Windows wordprocessing program.

- .WP means a WordPerfect version 5 file.

- .TXT means a text-only file. This is a file containing only text and standard computer codes such as tabs, carriage returns and line feeds, with no other special formatting (some word processor manuals refer to these text files as ASCII files). Most word processors can read these text files.

Users with Microsoft Word (MS-DOS) version 3.0 or later, should use the files with a .DOC filename extension; users with WordPerfect version 5.0 or later should use the files with a .WP extension. Users with different word processors (such as WordStar) should use the text files (the ASCII files with a filename extension of .TXT). If you use Microsoft Word in addition to another word processing program, we suggest you use the Microsoft Word files—they are the richest in terms of formatting and are the easiest to reformat.

Word for Windows users. PC users with Microsoft Word for Windows can use the Word for DOS files (the files with the .DOC filename extension). Word for Windows recognizes these as Word for DOS files and will convert them to the Word for Windows format.

3. Corporate Records Forms and Directory

The table below lists the corporate records forms included on the enclosed disk. These forms are used to document corporate decision-making and are covered with sample forms and instructions in Chapters 3 through 8.

Reminder

Each disk contains three versions of each form, each with a different filename extension as explained in Section A2, just above.

How to view the disk directory. If you want to view a directory of the names of the files included on the corporate records disk, do the following: Insert the disk in your A: drive. Type **DIR A:** to list the disk directory on the screen. Press **Cntrl S** to pause the scrolling of the display; type any key to continue the scrolling of the directory. If you have only one floppy disk drive, boot your computer with a system disk in your A: drive, replace the system disk with the corporate records disk, then type **DIR A:** to view the directory.

List of Corporate Records Files on the Disk

Filename	Document	Chapter	Section
MEETSUM	Meeting Summary Sheet	3	B, Step 2
CALL	Call of Meeting	3	B, Step 3
MEETLIST	Meeting Participant List	3	B, Step 4
NOTICE	Notice of Meeting	3	B, Step 5
ACKREC	Acknowledgment of Receipt of Notice of Meeting	3	B, Step 7
PROXY	Proxy	3	B, Step 8
MAILCERT	Certification of Mailing	3	B, Step 9
SHARANNL	Minutes of Annual Shareholders Meeting	5	A2
SHARSPCL	Minutes of Special Shareholders Meeting	5	B2
DIRANNL	Minutes of Annual Directors Meeting	6	B
DIRSPCL	Minutes of Special Directors Meeting	6	C
WAIVER	Waiver of Notice of Meeting	7	B, Step 1
APPROVE	Approval of Corporate Minutes by Directors or Shareholders	7	B, Step 3
PAPERLET	Cover Letter for Approval of Minutes of Paper Meeting	7	B, Step 4
CONSENT	Written Consent to Action Without Meeting	8	Step 2
REGFORM	Nolo Registration Form	10	D

B. How to Use the Disk

Most computer users know how to set up and use working disks and perform basic file opening and editing tasks with their word processor. If you are an experienced computer user, simply scan the information in this section, stopping at steps which appear helpful or informative. If you are just getting acquainted with your computer or word processor, the following steps should help you use the forms on the corporate records disk more efficiently.

Step 1. Make a Working Disk

Copy the set of files you wish to use from the original disk to a working disk.

a. PC With One Floppy Disk Drive

We don't recommend using the corporate records disk in a one-drive system, but if you do, here's how:

- Boot your computer with a system disk in drive A: (a system disk is one that has been formatted with the /S option). Your system disk should contain your word processing program and have enough room left for the file or files you wish to work with.

Note. Because of the limited disk space available on one floppy disk and the number of disk swaps which can occur when copying files on a one-drive system, we suggest you copy one or two files at a time to your working disk (as explained below) and repeat this process each time you wish to work with additional files.

- At the A:\> prompt, use the **COPY B:** command to transfer one or more files from the corporate records disk (we will pretend that this disk is in the B: drive) to your system disk in drive A:. DOS understands that a reference to the imaginary B: drive means that you will swap a different disk into the A: drive.

Example: To copy CONSENT.WP to your system disk, at the A:\> prompt, enter:

COPY CONSENT.WP B:

DOS will ask you to insert the diskette for Drive B:. Take the system disk out of Drive A: and replace it with the corporate records disk containing the CONSENT.WP file. Use the Directory command as explained in Section A3, above, to view the file directory on each disk.

DOS will copy the file to memory and ask you to insert the diskette for Drive A:. Replace the corporate records disk in Drive A: with your system disk and press any key. The file will be transferred from memory to your system disk. You may be asked to insert the source and target disks more than once depending on the amount of memory installed in your computer.

- Use the system disk containing your word processor and the copy of the transferred file as your working disk.

b. PC with Two Floppy Disk Drives

- Boot your computer with a system disk in drive A:. Your system disk should contain your word processing program.

- Place a blank floppy disk in drive B:. If necessary, format the blank disk by typing **FORMAT B:**

- Replace the system disk in drive A: with the original corporate records disk.

- At the A:\> prompt, use the COPY command to transfer the set of files you wish to work with from the original disk in drive A: to the blank disk in drive B:.

  - To copy the Word for DOS files, enter **COPY *.DOC B:**
  - To copy the WordPerfect files, enter **COPY *.WP B:**
  - To copy the Text files, enter **COPY *.TXT B:**

- Replace your system disk containing your word processing program in drive A:. Use the disk in drive B: as your working disk.

c. PC with Hard Disk Drive

- Boot your computer from the hard disk (turn on the computer without a floppy disk inserted in any drive).

- Place the original corporate records disk in drive A:.

- Type **PROMPT=PG** to tell DOS to display the current directory after the disk drive prompt on the screen.

- From the root directory of your hard disk (at the C:\> prompt), create a directory on the hard disk to hold your working files.

  Type **MD \CORP** to make the directory CORP on your hard disk.

- Make the CORP directory the current directory by typing **CD \CORP**.

- At the C:\CORP> prompt, copy the files you wish to work with from the original disk in drive A: to the CORP directory on the hard disk:

  To copy the Word files, enter **COPY A:*.DOC**
  To copy the WordPerfect files, enter **COPY A:*.WP**
  To copy the Text files, enter **COPY A:*.TXT**

- Use the CORP directory on your hard disk as your working directory. Whenever you wish to do this, type **CD \CORP** at the C:\> prompt.

Step 2. Open the File With Your Word Processing Program

Whenever you wish to use a corporate records form, open (some word processing manuals use the term "read" or "load") the form with your word processing (wp) program. If you use a word processor which cannot read one of the special document formats included on the disk—Microsoft Word and WordPerfect for the PC—use the text files (with a .TXT filename extension) included on the disk.

A Number of Word Processors Can Convert and Open Documents Created for Other Word Processors

Before using the text file versions of the files, check your word processor's manual to see if your program has a command for opening and converting documents written for Word or WordPerfect on the PC (some word processors are sold with separate conversion programs which do this). If your program has this ability, convert and use one of the document formats on the corporate records disk (namely, the Word or WordPerfect versions of the files) rather than the text versions of the files, as the document formats look better and are easier to use.

a. Opening Word or Word for Windows files

Files with a .DOC extension may be used with either Word for DOS or Word for Windows.

Word for DOS. Type **WORD** at the DOS prompt to run Word for DOS. Then select the Open command from the File menu. Next type the name of the .DOC file on your working corporate records disk or directory you wish to work with, then press **Enter** to open the file. If this file is not located on the current disk and directory, change the name of the current disk or directory listed at the top of the Open File dialog box to show the name of the disk or directory where the corporate records file is located. (See your Word manual for details.)

Word for Windows. Once you have Windows and the Word for Windows program running as explained in your program manuals, select the Open command from the Word for Windows File menu. Use the mouse to select the name of the .DOC file you wish to open after making sure that the current disk and directory containing this file is selected in the middle portion of the dialog box. A Convert File dialog box will appear with the Word for DOS item selected (to show that Word for Windows recognizes the corporate records disk as a Word for DOS file). Click the OK button to have Word for Windows convert and open the file. When you save the file, it will be saved in Word for Windows format—if you wish to preserve the format of the original Word for DOS corporate records file, use the Save As command to specify a new filename for the converted file. (See your manual for further information using the Save As command to rename and save Word for Windows files.)

b. Opening PC WordPerfect Files

Enter **WP filename** to run WordPerfect and retrieve (open) the file specified by filename. Alternatively, type **WP** to run the program, press any key to clear the screen, then press **Shift-F10** and type the name of the file to retrieve.

- If you enter **WP** to run WordPerfect and DOS responds with "Bad command or file name," this usually means that the WordPerfect program is located on another disk or in another directory. To run WordPerfect on drive A: from your working drive B:, type **A:WP** at the B:\> prompt. To run WordPerfect located in the \WP directory on your hard disk from the current \CORP directory, type **\WP** at the C:\CORP prompt.

- If you enter **Shift-F10** followed by a filename and **Return** to retrieve a file and WordPerfect responds with "File Not Found," this usually means that your working files are not contained in the current disk or hard disk directory used by WordPerfect. To change the current disk or hard disk directory from WordPerfect, press **F5**. At the bottom left of the screen you will see the disk and directory in use by WordPerfect. Type **=** , then type the disk and/or hard disk directory where your working files are located (for example, enter **B:** or **C:\CORP**). Then press **Return**. Exit the list files menu on the screen by pressing **0**. WordPerfect will then use this disk and/or hard disk directory to retrieve and save your files.

c. Opening Text Files With Another PC Word Processing Program

Most PC word processors will open text-only files (also called ASCII files). Text files are saved without any special formatting, so you may wish to center and bold heads or apply other formatting to each text file.

Example: WordStar 3.3 on the PC: Open the text file as a WS document by typing **WS filename** (**WS** *followed by a space then the filename of the text file). Another method is to run WordStar by typing* **WS**, *type* **d**, *then type the name of the text file. Set line spacing, justification, left and right margins, then press* **Cntrl-Q Cntrl-Q Cntrl-B** *to reformat the entire file. Press* **Cntrl-K Cntrl-S** *to save the reformatted WordStar document.*

Make sure WordStar knows where to find and save your files:

• If the WordStar program is on the disk in drive A: and your working disk is in drive B:, start WordStar from your B: drive by typing **A:WS** at the B:\> prompt.

• Another way to log on to your working disk is to press **Cntrl-K Cntrl-L** from WordStar's No File menu (the menu listed when you start WordStar or quit a file), then type **B:** followed by a **Return**. If you wish to log on to a different disk drive while editing a file, press **Cntrl-K Cntrl-L**, then type **B:** followed by **Return**.

Note for hard disk users. WordStar 3.3 only works well on files contained in the current directory. If you do not have WordStar or your corporate records files are not in the root directory (if either is inside a separate directory on your hard disk), you will need to copy your corporate records files into your WordStar directory or copy WS.COM, WSMSGS.OVR and WSOVLY1.OVR to your \CORP directory before running WordStar. For examples of the copy command for hard disk users, see Step 1, above.

Step 3. Fill in the Blanks on the Form

When completing the corporate records forms on disk, the only work required is to find and fill in each blank in the form according to the specific instructions contained in the incorporation steps in the preceding chapters.

Each blank item in a file is marked by a series of underline characters. To quickly find each blank, use your word processor's search command to go to the next blank by searching for an underline **(Shift -)** character.

Example (Searching in PC WordStar): Type **Cntrl-Q Cntrl-F**, *then type an underline character (__), then press* **Return** *to begin the search. To repeat the search for another underline, type* **Cntrl-L**.

After finding a blank, select it and replace it with the appropriate information, following the specific instructions and sample forms contained in the appropriate chapter in this book.

Standard formatting styles have been applied to the files on the disk to keep your work to a minimum. If you wish to make changes to these styles, please read Section C, below.

Step 4. Print the File

Fill in all blanks in your corporate records file, deleting any unused blanks or inserting "N/A" or "Not Applicable" in any blanks that don't apply in the final version of the file. Next, print the form from your word processor. There are no specific legal or regulatory requirements for formatting or printing the forms on the disk. We suggest that all forms be printed on letter-sized (8½" x 11") paper since this is the standard size accepted by most corporate records books.

Save your Work

Remember to save your work after printing and before quitting the current editing session. Use the appropriate menu or keystroke save command from your word processor.

Example 1 (Word for DOS): Choose **Save (Alt-Shift-F2)** *or* **Save As (Alt-F2)** *from the File menu.*

Example 2 (Word for Windows): Choose **Save (Shift-F12)** *or* **Save As (F12)** *from the File menu.*

Example 3 (PC WordPerfect): Press **F10** *to save the current file and keep the document in memory and on the screen. Alternatively, press* **F7** *and type* **Y** *to save the file. Then type* **Y** *to exit the program or* **N** *to clear the screen and work with another file.*

Example 4 (PC WordStar): Type **Cntrl-K Cntrl-S** *to save the current file and keep the document in memory and on the screen. Type* **Cntrl-K Cntrl-Q** *to leave the saved document and open another document. Type* **Cntrl-K Cntrl-X** *to save the current file and exit WordStar.*

C. Document Formats

We've kept the general format of each document as simple and clean as possible: heads are bold and centered; body text paragraphs are marked with a single first line indent or tab. Below is brief description of the formats used with each PC document.

1. Word Document Format

Word documents end with a .DOC filename extension. Formatting used for the files are basic and can be changed using Word's Define Styles command (see your manual). Titles and section headings for corporate records forms are centered and boldfaced.

Standard typesetting document formatting was used in these files, including:

- single-spacing after all punctuation

- one return after each paragraph, and

- tabs only if necessary for special alignment or indentation.

Also, the body text for all letters is left justified (no first-line paragraph indent.

Word document formatting should be adjusted by adding spacing before and after paragraphs with the Paragraph command from the Format menu; indents should be set from the ruler or with the Paragraph command.

2. WordPerfect Document Format

WordPerfect documents (those with a .WP filename extension) are produced with the same formats as Word documents (see above).

3. Text-Only File Format

Text-only (ASCII) files with a .TXT filename extension have the text format expected by most PC word processors with double-spacing (two pairs of Carriage Return/Line Feed codes) at the end of each paragraph.

Note. A line of ^@'s (a string of 0's) may appear as the last line of the text files. If so, delete this line prior to saving the text file as a word processing document.

D. Registration Form

We hope you are pleased with this book-with-disk product. If you complete the tear-out Registration Form included at the back of this book (we pay postage) we will add your name to our mailing list and notify you of future updates to our corporate records disks, publications and programs. You will also receive a free two-year subscription to the *Nolo News*, a legal self-help newspaper that contains news of legal changes and updates to all Nolo publications. We promise never to sell or give your name and address to anyone else.

Registration Form on Disk

Instead of filling in the tear-out registration form, computer users may wish to complete the registration form included in the REGFORM file on the disk. As usual, this form is provided in three file formats (.DOC, .WP and .TXT).

Corporate Filing Offices

Alabama

Secretary of State
Corporations Division
State Office Building, Room 524
Montgomery, AL 36130

Alaska

Department of Commerce and Economic
Development
Corporations Section
P.O. Box D
Juneau, AK 99811

Arizona

Corporation Commission
P.O. Box 6019
Phoenix, AZ 85005[1]

Arkansas

Secretary of State
Corporations Section
State Capitol Building, Room 058
Little Rock, AR 72201

California

Secretary of State
Corporate Division
1230 J Street
Sacramento, CA 95814[1]

Colorado

Secretary of State
Corporations Office
1560 Broadway, Suite 200
Denver, CO 80202

Connecticut

Secretary of State
30 Trinity Street,
Hartford, CT 06106

Delaware

Department of State
Division of Corporations
P.O. Box 898
Dover, DE 19903

District of Columbia

Dept. of Consumer and Regulatory Affairs
Corporations Division
614 H St., NW
Washington, DC 20001

Florida

Department of State
Division of Corporations
P.O. Box 6327
Tallahassee, FL 32314

Georgia

Secretary of State
Business Services and Regulation
Suite 315, West Tower
2 Martin Luther King, Jr. Drive, SE
Atlanta, GA 30334

Hawaii

Department of Business and Consumer Affairs
Business Registration Division
P.O. Box 40
Honolulu, HI 96810

---

[1]Filings may also be permitted by mail or in person at branch offices in Tucson, AZ; Los Angeles, San Diego and San Francisco, CA; Chicago, IL.

Idaho

Secretary of State
Statehouse, Room 203
Boise, ID 83720

Illinois

Secretary of State
Corporation Department
328 Centennial Building
Springfield, IL 62756 *

Indiana

Secretary of State
Corporations Division
Room 155, State House
Indianapolis, IN 46204

Iowa

Secretary of State
Corporations Division
2nd Floor, Hoover Building
Des Moines, IA 50319

Kansas

Secretary of State
Corporation Division
2nd Floor, State Capitol
Topeka, KS 66612

Kentucky

Secretary of State
State Capitol
P.O. Box 718
Frankfort, KY 40602

Louisiana

Secretary of State
Corporations Division
P.O. Box 94125
Baton Rouge, LA 70804

Maine

Secretary of State
Bureau of Corporations, Elections and
Commissions
State House Station #101
Augusta, ME 04333

Maryland

Department of Assessments and Taxation
Corporate Charter Division
310 West Preston Street
Baltimore, MD 21201

Massachusetts

Secretary of State
Corporations Division
One Ashburton Place, Room 1717
Boston, MA 02108

Michigan

Department of Commerce
Corporation & Securities Bureau
Corporation Division
P.O. Box 30054
Lansing, MI 48909

Minnesota

Secretary of State
Business Services Division
180 State Office Building
St. Paul, MN 55155

Mississippi

Secretary of State
Corporate Division
P.O. Box 136
Jackson, MS 39205

Missouri

Secretary of State
Corporations Division
P.O. Box 778
Jefferson City, MO 65102

Montana

Secretary of State
Corporation Bureau
Montana State Capitol
Helena, MT 59620

Nebraska

Secretary of State
Corporate Office
Suite 2304, State Capitol Building
Lincoln, NE 68509

Nevada

Secretary of State
Capitol Complex
Carson City, NV 89710

New Hampshire

Secretary of State
Corporation Division
Room 204, State House
Concord, NH 03301

New Jersey

Department of State
Division of Commercial Recording
CN 308
Trenton, NJ 08625

New Mexico

State Corporation Commission
Corporation Department
P.O. Drawer 1269
Santa Fe, NM 87504

New York

Department of State
Division of Corporations
162 Washington Avenue
Albany, NY 12231

North Carolina

Department of the Secretary of State
Corporations Division
300 North Salisbury Street
Raleigh, NC 27603

North Dakota

Secretary of State
Corporations Division
Main Capitol Building
600 East Boulevard Avenue
Bismarck, ND 58505

Ohio

Secretary of State
Corporations Section
30 East Broad Street, 14th Floor
Columbus, OH 43266

Oklahoma

Secretary of State
Corporate Filing Division
101 State Capitol Building
Oklahoma City, OK 73105

Oregon

Secretary of State
Corporation Division
158 12th Street NE
Salem, OR 97310

Pennsylvania

Department of State
Corporation Bureau
Room 308, North Office Building
Harrisburg, PA 17120

Rhode Island

Secretary of State
Corporations Division
100 North Main Street
Providence, RI 02903

South Carolina

Secretary of State
Corporations Department
P.O. Box 11350
Columbia, SC 29211

South Dakota

Secretary of State
State Capitol
500 E. Capitol
Pierre, SD 57501

Tennessee

Secretary of State
Corporations Section
18th Floor, James K. Polk Building
Nashville, TN 37219

Texas

Secretary of State
Statutory Filings Division
Corporations Section
P.O. Box 13697
Austin, TX 78711

Utah

Department of Commerce
Division of Corporations and
Commercial Code
P.O. Box 45801
Salt Lake City, UT 84145

Vermont

Secretary of State
Corporations Division
Pavilion Office Building
Montpelier, VT 05602

Virginia

State Corporation Commission
Clerk's Office
P.O. Box 1197
Richmond, VA 23209

Washington

Secretary of State
Corporations Division
2nd Floor Republic Building
505 E. Union
Olympia, WA 98504

West Virginia

Secretary of State
Corporations Division
State Capitol, W-139
Charleston, WV 25305

Wisconsin

Secretary of State
Corporation Division
P.O. Box 7846
Madison, WI 53707

Wyoming

Secretary of State
Corporations Division
Capitol Building
Cheyenne, WY 82002

State Business Corporation Statutes

Many state corporate filing offices provide copies of the state's corporation statutes for free or a minimal charge. Also, you may be able to find a compact edition of your state's corporation code or business corporation act in a local legal bookstore. If not, West Publishing Company carries individual compact corporation code volumes for the states of California, Minnesota, Oklahoma, Pennsylvania and Texas (and possibly others—call 800 information for West Publishing to talk to Customer Service). Of course your local county law library will have one or more reference editions of your state's corporation code. (For more on legal research, see Chapter 1, Section D and Chapter 9, Section C.).

State Corporation Law	Name of Code Volume	Sections
Alabama Business Corporation Act	Alabama Code (Title 10-2A)	10-2A-1 to 10-2A-339
Alaska Corporations Code	Alaska Statutes	10.05.003 to 10.05.828
Arizona Business Corporation Act	Arizona Revised Statutes Annotated (Title 10)	10-002 to 10-150
Arkansas Business Corporation Act	Arkansas Statutes Annotated	4-27-101 to 4-27-1706
California General Corporation Law	California Corporations Code	100 to 2319
Colorado Corporation Code	Colorado Revised Statutes (Title 7, Vol. 3A)	7-1-101 to 7-10-113
Connecticut Stock Corporation Act	Connecticut General Statutes Annotated	33-282 to 33-418
Delaware General Corporation Law	Delaware Code Annotated	101 to 398
District of Columbia Business Corporation Act	District of Columbia Code Annotated	29-301 to 29-399.51
Florida General Corporation Act	Florida Statutes Annotated—Chapter 607	607.001 to 607.414
Georgia Business Corporation Code	Georgia Code Annotated	14-2-1 to 14-2-411
Hawaii Business Corporation Act	Hawaii Revised Statutes	415-1 to 418-24
Idaho Business Corporation Act	Idaho Code	30-1-1 to 30-1-152
Illinois Business Corporation Act	Illinois Annotated Statutes—Chapter 32	§§ 1.01 to 17.05
Indiana Business Corporation Law	Indiana Code Annotated	23-1-17-1; 23-1-54-2; 23-3-1-1 to 23-3-7-1
Iowa Business Corporation Act	Iowa Code Annotated	490.101 to 490.1704
Kansas General Corporation Code	Kansas Statutes Annotated Volumes 2 & 2A	17-6001 to 17-7404
Kentucky Business Corporation Act	Kentucky Revised Statutes Annotated	271A.005 to 271A.710
Louisiana Business Corporation Law	Louisiana Revised Statutes Annotated	12:1 to 12:178; 12:301 to 12:321
Maine Business Corporation Act	Maine Revised Statutes Annotated Title 13A	101 to 1404
Maryland General Corporation Law	Maryland Corporations & Associations Code Annotated	1-101 to 3-603; 7-101 to 7-305

State Corporation Law	Name of Code Volume	Sections
Massachusetts Business Corporation Law	Massachusetts General Laws Annotated —Chapter 156B—Chapter 181	1 to 115 1 to 23
Michigan Business Corporation Act	Michigan Compiled Laws Annotated	450.1101 to 450-2064
Minnesota Business Corporation Act	Minnesota Statutes Annotated (Chapter 302A)	302A.001 to 302A-917; 303.01 to 303.25
Mississippi Business Corporation Act	Mississippi Code Annotated	79-3-1 to 79-3-293
Missouri General and Business Corporation Law	Missouri Annotated Statutes	351.010 to 351.720
Montana Business Corporation Act	Montana Code Annotated (Title 35, Chapter 1)	35-1-101 to 35-1-1306
Nebraska Business Corporation Act	Nebraska Revised Statutes	21-2001 to 21-20144
Nevada General Corporation Law	Nevada Revised Statutes	78.101 to 78.790; 80.005 to 80.240
New Hampshire Business Corporation Act	New Hampshire Revised Statutes Annotated	293-A:1 to 293-A:156
New Jersey Business Corporation Act	New Jersey Statutes Annotated	14A:1-1 to 14A:16-4
New Mexico Business Corporation Act	New Mexico Statutes Annotated	53-11-1 to 53-18-12
New York Business Corporation Law	New York Business Corporation Law	101 to 2001
North Carolina Business Corporation Act	North Carolina General Statutes	55-1 to 55-176
North Dakota Business Corporation Act	North Dakota Century Code	10-19.1-01 to 10-23-19
Ohio General Corporation Law	Ohio Revised Code Annotated	1701.01 to 1701.99; 1703.01 to 1703.99
Oklahoma General Corporation Act	Oklahoma Statutes Annotated—Title 18	1001 to 1143
Oregon Business Corporation Act	Oregon Revised Statutes (Chapter 60)	60.001 to 60.967
Pennsylvania Business Corporation Law	Pennsylvania Statutes Annotated—Title 18	1001to 2204
Rhode Island Business Corporation Act	Rhode Island General Laws	7-1.1-1 to 7-1.1-141
South Carolina Business Corporation Act	South Carolina Code	33-1-10 to 33-29-30

State Corporation Law	Name of Code Volume	Sections
South Dakota Business Corporation Act	South Dakota Compiled Laws Annotated	47-1-101 to 47-9-20
Tennessee Business Corporation Act	Tennessee Code Annotated	48-1-101 to 48-17-103
Texas Business Corporation Act	Texas Business Corporation Act Annotated	Articles 1.01 to 11.01
	Texas Revised Civil Statutes Annotated	Articles 1302-1.01 to 1302-7.05
Utah Business Corporation Act	Utah Code Annotated	16-10-1 to 16-10-143
Vermont Business Corporation Act	Vermont Statutes Annotated—Title II	1801 to 2216
Virginia Stock Corporation Act	Virginia Code	13-1-601 to 13-1-998; 56 to 249-7
Washington Business Corporation Act	Washington Revised Code Annotated	23A.04.010 to 23A.98.050
West Virginia Corporation Act	West Virginia Code	31-1-1 to 31-1-160
Wisconsin Business Corporation Law	Wisconsin Statutes Annotated	180.01 to 180.97

APPENDIX C

Tear-Out Corporate Records Forms

Form	Chapter	Filename
Meeting Summary Sheet	3	MEETSUM
Call of Meeting	3	CALL
Meeting Participant List	3	MEETLIST
Notice of Meeting	3	NOTICE
Acknowledgment of Receipt of Notice of Meeting	3	ACKREC
Proxy	3	PROXY
Certification of Mailing	3	MAILCERT
Minutes of Annual Shareholders Meeting	5	SHARANNL
Minutes of Special Shareholders Meeting	5	SHARSPCL
Minutes of Annual Directors Meeting	6	DIRANNL
Minutes of Special Directors Meeting	6	DIRSPCL
Waiver of Notice of Meeting	7	WAIVER
Approval of Corporate Minutes by Directors or Shareholders	7	APPROVE
Cover Letter for Approval of Minutes of Paper Meeting	7	PAPERLET
Written Consent to Action Without Meeting	8	CONSENT

MEETING SUMMARY SHEET

Name of Corporation:

_____

Year: 19_____

Type of Meeting: ☐ Annual/Regular or ☐ Special
Meeting of: ☐ Directors or ☐ Shareholders

Date: _____, 19_____ Time: _____:_____ _____.M.

Place: _____

Meeting Called By: _____

Purpose: _____

_____

Committee or Other Reports or Presentations: _____

Other Reminders or Notes: _____

Notice Required: ☐ Written ☐ Verbal ☐ Not Required

Notice Must Be Given By Date: _____

Notice of Meeting Given To:

Name	Type of Notice*	Location or Phone Number	Date Notice Given	Date Acknowledged Receipt

*Types of Notice: Written (mailed, hand-delivered); Verbal (in-person, telephone conversation, answering machine, voice mail); e-mail; Fax.

CALL OF MEETING

To:

Secretary: _____

Corporation: _____

Corporation Address: _____

_____

The following person(s):

Name	Title	No. Shares
_____	_____	_____
_____	_____	_____
_____	_____	_____

authorized under provisions of the Bylaws of _____,

hereby make(s) a call and request to hold a(n) _____ meeting

of the _____ of the corporation for the purpose(s) of:

_____

_____

_____.

The date and time of the meeting requested is: _____

_____.

The requested location for the meeting is _____

_____,

state of _____.

The Secretary is requested to provide all proper notices as required by the Bylaws of the corporation and any other necessary materials to all persons entitled to attend the meeting.

Date: _____

Signed: _____

MEETING PARTICIPANT LIST

Name of Corporation:

_____

Type of Meeting: ☐ Annual/Regular or ☐ Special

Meeting of: ☐ Directors or ☐ Shareholders

Meeting Date: _____, 19____

Meeting Participants *(list names in alphabetical order):*

Name: _____

Address: _____

_____ Telephone: _____

☐ Director

☐ Shareholder: Number and Type of Shares: _____

☐ Officer: Title _____

☐ Other (position and reason for attendance): _____

Name: _____

Address: _____

_____ Telephone: _____

☐ Director

☐ Shareholder: Number and Type of Shares: _____

☐ Officer: Title _____

☐ Other (position and reason for attendance): _____

Name: _____

Address: _____

_____ Telephone: _____

☐ Director

☐ Shareholder: Number and Type of Shares: _____

☐ Officer: Title _____

☐ Other (position and reason for attendance): _____

Name: _____

Address: _____

_____ Telephone: _____

☐ Director

☐ Shareholder: Number and Type of Shares: _____

☐ Officer: Title _____

☐ Other (position and reason for attendance): _____

Name: _____

Address: _____

_____ Telephone: _____

☐ Director

☐ Shareholder: Number and Type of Shares: _____

☐ Officer: Title _____

☐ Other (position and reason for attendance): _____

Name: _____

Address: _____

_____ Telephone: _____

☐ Director

☐ Shareholder: Number and Type of Shares: _____

☐ Officer: Title _____

☐ Other (position and reason for attendance): _____

Name: _____

Address: _____

_____ Telephone: _____

☐ Director

☐ Shareholder: Number and Type of Shares: _____

☐ Officer: Title _____

☐ Other (position and reason for attendance): _____

Name: _____

Address: _____

_____ Telephone: _____

☐ Director

☐ Shareholder: Number and Type of Shares: _____

☐ Officer: Title _____

☐ Other (position and reason for attendance): _____

Name: _____

Address: _____

_____ Telephone: _____

☐ Director

☐ Shareholder: Number and Type of Shares: _____

☐ Officer: Title _____

☐ Other (position and reason for attendance): _____

Name: _____

Address: _____

_____ Telephone: _____

☐ Director

☐ Shareholder: Number and Type of Shares: _____

☐ Officer: Title _____

☐ Other (position and reason for attendance): _____

Name: _____

Address: _____

_____ Telephone: _____

☐ Director

☐ Shareholder: Number and Type of Shares: _____

☐ Officer: Title _____

☐ Other (position and reason for attendance): _____

NOTICE OF MEETING OF

_____

A(n) _____ meeting of the _____ of

_____ will be held at

_____,

state of _____, on _____, 19___ at ___:___ __.M.

The purpose(s) of the meeting is/are as follows:

_____

_____

_____.

If you are a shareholder and cannot attend the meeting and wish to designate another person to vote your shares for you, please deliver a signed proxy form to the secretary of the corporation before the meeting. Contact the secretary if you need help obtaining or preparing this form.

_____
Signature of Secretary

Name of Secretary: _____

Corporation: _____

Address: _____

Phone: _____ Fax: _____

ACKNOWLEDGMENT OF RECEIPT OF NOTICE OF MEETING

I received notice of a(n) _____ meeting of the

_____ of _____

on _____, 19___. The notice of meeting stated the date, time, place and

purpose of the upcoming meeting.

The notice of meeting was:

☐ received by fax, telephone number _____

☐ delivered orally to me in person

☐ delivered orally to me by phone call, telephone number _____

☐ left in a message on an answering machine or voice mail, telephone number

_____

☐ delivered by mail to _____

☐ delivered via e-mail, PIN number _____

☐ other: _____

Dated: _____

Signed: _____

Printed Name: _____

Please return to:

Name: _____

Corporation: _____

Address: _____

Phone: _____ Fax: _____

PROXY

The undersigned shareholder, of _____

_____, authorizes

_____ to act as his/her proxy and to

represent and vote his/her shares at a(n) _____ meeting of

shareholders to be held at _____

_____, state of _____,

on _____, 19___ at ___:___ __.M.

Dated: _____

Signature of Shareholder: _____

Printed Name of Shareholder: _____

Please return proxy by _____, 19_____ to:

Name: _____

Title: _____

Corporation: _____

Address: _____

City, State, Zip: _____

Fax: _____ Phone: _____

CERTIFICATION OF MAILING

I, the undersigned acting secretary of _____,
hereby certify that I caused notice of the _____ meeting of the
_____ of _____,
to be held on _____, 19____, to be deposited in the United States
mail, postage prepaid, on _____, 19____, addressed to the
_____ of the corporation at their most recent addresses as shown

☐ on the books of this corporation

☐ as follows:

A true and correct copy of such notice is attached to this certificate.

Dated: _____

Signed: _____

Printed Name: _____

☐ Director

☐ Shareholder: Number and Type of Shares: _____

☐ Officer: Title _____

☐ Other (position and reason for attendance): _____

MINUTES OF THE ANNUAL MEETING OF SHAREHOLDERS OF

_____

An annual meeting of the shareholders of the corporation was held on

_____, 19____ at ____:____ __.M., at _____

_____, state of _____,

for the purpose of electing the directors of the corporation and for the transaction of any other

business that may properly come before the meeting, including

_____

_____.

_____ acted as chairperson, and

_____ acted as secretary of the meeting.

The chairperson called the meeting to order.

The secretary announced that the meeting was called by _____

_____.

The secretary announced that the meeting was held pursuant to notice, if and as required

under the Bylaws of this corporation, or that notice had been waived by all shareholders entitled

to receive notice under the Bylaws. Copies of any certificates of mailing of notice prepared by

the secretary of the corporation and any written waivers signed by shareholders entitled to

receive notice of this meeting were attached to these minutes by the secretary.

The secretary announced that an alphabetical list of the names and numbers of shares

held by all shareholders of the corporation was available and open to inspection by any person

in attendance at the meeting.

The secretary announced that there were present, in person or by proxy, representing a

quorum of the shareholders, the following shareholders, proxyholders and shares:

Name   Number of Shares

_____   _____

_____   _____

_____   _____

_____   _____

_____   _____

_____   _____

The secretary attached written proxy statements, executed by the appropriate shareholders, to these minutes for any shares listed above as held by a proxyholder.

The following persons were also present at the meeting:

Name   Title

_____   _____

_____   _____

_____   _____

_____   _____

_____   _____

The secretary announced that the minutes of the _____

meeting held on _____, 19_____

☐ had been distributed prior to

☐ were distributed at

☐ were read at

the meeting. After discussion, a vote was taken and the minutes of the meeting were approved by the shares in attendance.

The following annual and special reports were presented at the meeting by the following persons:

_____

_____

_____.

The chairperson announced that the next item of business was the nomination and election of the board of directors for another _____ term of office. The following nominations were made and seconded:

Name(s) of Nominee(s)

_____

_____

_____

_____

_____

The secretary next took the votes of shareholders entitled to vote for the election of directors at the meeting, and, after counting the votes, announced that the following persons were elected to serve on the Board of Directors of this corporation for another term of office:

Names of Board Members

_____

_____

_____

_____

_____

On motion duly made and carried by the affirmative vote of _____ shareholders in attendance at the meeting, the following resolutions were adopted by shareholders entitled to vote at the meeting:

There being no further business to come before the meeting, it was adjourned on motion duly made and carried.

_____
_____, Secretary

MINUTES OF SPECIAL MEETING OF SHAREHOLDERS OF

_____

A special meeting of the shareholders of the corporation was held on

_____, 19_____ at ____:____ __.M., at

_____,

state of _____, for the purpose(s) of

_____

_____

_____.

_____ acted as chairperson, and

_____ acted as secretary of the meeting.

The chairperson called the meeting to order.

The secretary announced that the meeting was called by _____

_____.

The secretary announced that the meeting was held pursuant to notice, if and as required under the Bylaws of this corporation, or that notice had been waived by all shareholders entitled to receive notice under the Bylaws. Copies of any certificates of mailing of notice prepared by the secretary of the corporation and any written waivers signed by shareholders entitled to receive notice of this meeting were attached to these minutes by the secretary.

The secretary announced that an alphabetical list of the names and numbers of shares held by all shareholders of the corporation was available and open to inspection by any person in attendance at the meeting.

The secretary announced that there were present, in person or by proxy, representing a quorum of the shareholders, the following shareholders, proxyholders and shares:

Name   Number of Shares

_____   _____

_____   _____

_____   _____

_____   _____

The secretary attached written proxy statements, executed by the appropriate shareholders, to these minutes for any shares listed above as held by a proxyholder.

The following persons were also present at the meeting:

Name   Title

_____   _____

_____   _____

_____   _____

_____   _____

_____   _____

The secretary announced that the minutes of the _____

meeting held on _____, 19____

☐ had been distributed prior to

☐ were distributed at

☐ were read at

the meeting. After discussion, a vote was taken and the minutes of the meeting were approved by the shares in attendance.

The following reports were presented at the meeting by the following persons:

_____

_____

_____

_____

_____.

On motion duly made and carried by the affirmative vote of _____ shareholders in attendance at the meeting, the following resolutions were adopted by shareholders entitled to vote at the meeting:

There being no further business to come before the meeting, it was adjourned on motion duly made and carried.

_____
_____, Secretary

MINUTES OF THE ANNUAL MEETING OF DIRECTORS OF

_____

An annual meeting of the directors of the corporation was held on

_____, 19_____ at _____:_____ ___.M., at

_____, state

of _____, for the purpose of reviewing the prior

year's business, discussing corporate operations for the upcoming year, and for the transaction

of any other business that may properly come before the meeting, including

_____

_____

_____

_____.

_____ acted as chairperson, and

_____ acted as secretary of the meeting.

The chairperson called the meeting to order.

The secretary announced that the meeting was called by

_____.

The secretary announced that the meeting was held pursuant to notice, if and as required under the Bylaws of this corporation, or that notice had been waived by all directors entitled to receive notice under the Bylaws. Copies of any certificates of mailing of notice prepared by the secretary of the corporation and any written waivers signed by directors entitled to receive notice of this meeting were attached to these minutes by the secretary.

The secretary announced that the following directors were present at the meeting:

Name of Director

_____

_____

_____

_____

_____

_____

The above directors, having been elected to serve on the board for another
_____ term by the shareholders at an annual meeting of shareholders held
on _____, 19_____, accepted their positions on the board. The
secretary then announced that the presence of these directors at the meeting represented a
quorum of the board of directors as defined in the Bylaws of this corporation.

The following persons were also present at the meeting:

Name   Title

_____   _____

_____   _____

_____   _____

_____   _____

_____   _____

The secretary announced that the minutes of the _____ meeting
held on _____, 19_____

☐ had been distributed prior to

☐ were distributed at

☐ were read at

the meeting. After discussion, a vote was taken and the minutes of the meeting were approved by
the directors in attendance.

The following reports were presented at the meeting by the following persons:

_____

_____

_____.

The chairperson announced that the next item of business was the appointment of the
officers and of standing committee members of the corporation to another _____
term of office. After discussion, the following persons were appointed to serve in the following
capacities as officers, committee members or in other roles in the service of the corporation for
the upcoming year:

Name   Title

_____   _____

_____   _____

_____   _____

_____   _____

_____   _____

The next item of business was the determination of compensation or fringe benefits to be paid or awarded for services rendered the corporation by employees and staff. After discussion, the following employee compensation amounts were approved by the board to be paid for the upcoming fiscal year to the following employees of the corporation:

Name   Type and Amount of
                                                        Compensation or Benefit

_____   _____

_____   _____

_____   _____

_____   _____

_____   _____

On motion duly made and carried by the affirmative vote of _____ directors in attendance at the meeting, the following resolutions were adopted by directors entitled to vote at the meeting:

There being no further business to come before the meeting, it was adjourned on motion duly made and carried.

_____

_____, Secretary

MINUTES OF SPECIAL MEETING OF DIRECTORS OF

_____

An special meeting of the directors of the corporation was held on

_____, 19___ at ___:___ __.M., at

_____,

state of _____, for the purpose(s) of

_____

_____

_____

_____.

_____ acted as chairperson, and

_____ acted as secretary of the meeting.

The chairperson called the meeting to order.

The secretary announced that the meeting was called by _____

_____.

The secretary announced that the meeting was held pursuant to notice, if and as required under the Bylaws of this corporation, or that notice had been waived by all directors entitled to receive notice under the Bylaws. Copies of any certificates of mailing of notice prepared by the secretary of the corporation and any written waivers signed by directors entitled to receive notice of this meeting were attached to these minutes by the secretary.

The secretary announced that the following directors were present at the meeting, representing a quorum of the board of directors:

Name of Director

_____

_____

_____

_____

_____

The following persons were also present at the meeting:

Name   Title

_____   _____

_____   _____

_____   _____

_____   _____

_____   _____

The secretary announced that the minutes of the _____

meeting held on _____, 19____.

☐ had been distributed prior to

☐ were distributed at

☐ were read at

the meeting. After discussion, a vote was taken and the minutes of the meeting were approved by

the directors in attendance.

The following reports were presented at the meeting by the following persons:

_____

_____

_____

_____

_____.

The secretary announced that the next item of business was the consideration of one or

more formal resolutions for approval by the board. After introduction and discussion, and upon

motion duly made and carried by the affirmative vote of _____

directors in attendance at the meeting, the following resolutions were adopted by directors

entitled to vote at the meeting:

There being no further business to come before the meeting, it was adjourned on motion duly made and carried.

_____

_____, Secretary

WAIVER OF NOTICE OF MEETING OF

_____

The undersigned _____ waive(s) notice of and

consent(s) to the holding of the _____ meeting of the

_____ of _____

_____ held at

_____, state of

_____, on _____, 19____ at ____:____ ___.M.,

for the purpose(s) of:

_____

_____

_____

_____

_____.

Dated: _____

Signature   Printed Name

_____   _____

_____   _____

_____   _____

_____   _____

_____   _____

Date: _____

Name: _____

Mailing Address: _____

City, State, Zip: _____

Re: Approval of Minutes

Dear _____:

    I am enclosing minutes of a meeting of the _____ of _____ that show approval of one or more specific resolutions. Each resolution contains the language of an item of business approved by the _____ in the past.

    Since these items were agreeable to the _____, we did not hold a formal meeting to approve these decisions. We are now finalizing our corporate records and preparing formal minutes that reflect prior corporate decisions.

    To confirm that these minutes accurately reflect the past decisions reached by the _____, please date and sign the enclosed Approval of Corporate Minutes form and mail it to me at the address below. If you have corrections or additions to suggest, please contact me so we can hold a meeting or make other arrangements for formalizing and documenting these changes.

Sincerely,

_____

Enclosures: Minutes and Approval of Corporate Minutes Forms

Please return to:

Name: _____

Corporation: _____

Mailing Address: _____

City, State, Zip: _____

Phone: _____ Fax: _____

APPROVAL OF CORPORATE MINUTES OF

_____

The undersigned _____ consent(s) to the minutes of

the _____ meeting of the _____

of _____

held at _____,

state of _____, on _____, 19____ at ____:____ __.M.,

attached to this form, and accept(s) the resolutions passed and decisions made at such meeting

as valid and binding acts of the _____ of the corporation.

Dated: _____

Signature   Printed Name

_____   _____

_____   _____

_____   _____

_____   _____

_____   _____

WRITTEN CONSENT TO ACTION WITHOUT MEETING

The undersigned _____ of

_____ hereby consent(s) as follows:

_____

_____

_____

_____

_____

_____

_____.

Dated: _____

Signature   Printed Name

_____   _____

_____   _____

_____   _____

_____   _____

_____   _____

Index

F

Family-run corporation, corporate meeting, 3/3
File, opening, 10/9-11
File types, 10/4
Filing offices, 1/8-9
    state-by-state listing of, Appendix A
Floppy disk drive
    PC with one, making working disk, 10/6-7
    PC with tng working disk, 10/8
Florida
    corporate filing office, Appendix A
    corporation statutes, Appendix A
Folder, for corporate meeting, 3/4
Format, disk, 10/3
Forms
    filling in blanks, on computer, 10/12
    records, Appendix C

G

Georgia
    corporate filing office, Appendix A
    corporation statutes, Appendix A

H

Hard disk drive, PC with, making working disk, 10/8
Hawaii
    corporate filing office, Appendix A
    corporation statutes, Appendix B

I

Idaho
    corporate filing office, Appendix A
    corporation statutes, Appendix B
Illinois
    corporate filing office, Appendix A
    corporation statutes, Appendix B
Indiana
    corporate filing office, Appendix A
    corporation statutes, Appendix B
Information packet
    distribution of, 3/33-36
    pre-corporate meeting, 3/27-28
Iowa
    corporate filing office, Appendix A
    corporation statutes, Appendix B

K

Kansas
    corporate filing office, Appendix A
    corporation statutes, Appendix B
Kentucky
    corporate filing office, Appendix A
    corporation statutes, Appendix B

L

Law
    researching, 1/10-15
        Blue Sky Law, 1/15
        Commercial Code, 1/15
        Revenue Code, 1/15
        Securities Act, 1/15
        state corporate statute, how to find, 1/11-12
        state corporations code, how to find, 1/12-15
        Tax Code, 1/15
    state, for corporations, Appendix B
Lawyer
    cost of services, 9/5-7
        charging structure, 9/7
        use of nonlawyer professionals, 9/6
    locating, 9/2-8
    tax advice from, 9/4
Legal research, doing own, 9/10-14
Legislation, state, for corporations, Appendix B
List of participants, corporate meeting, 3/16-19
    sample, 3/17
List of shareholders, availability at corporate meeting, 3/18
Louisiana
    corporate filing office, Appendix A
    corporation statutes, Appendix B

M

Mailing, notice, certification of, 3/35-36
    sample, 3/36
Maine
    corporate filing office, Appendix A
    corporation statutes, Appendix B
Maryland
    corporate filing office, Appendix A
    corporation statutes, Appendix B
Massachusetts
    corporate filing office, Appendix A

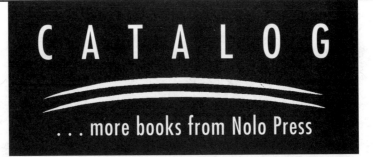

CATALOG

... more books from Nolo Press

ESTATE PLANNING & PROBATE

Make Your Own Living Trust, Clifford	1st Ed	$19.95	LITR
Plan Your Estate With a Living Trust, Clifford	3rd Ed	$24.95	NEST
Nolo's Simple Will Book, Clifford	2nd Ed	$17.95	SWIL
Who Will Handle Your Finances If You Can't?, Clifford & Randolph	1st Ed	$19.95	FINA
The Conservatorship Book (California), Goldoftas & Farren	2nd Ed	$29.95	CNSV
How to Probate an Estate (California), Nissley	7th Ed	$34.95	PAE
Nolo's Law Form Kit: Wills, Clifford & Goldoftas	1st Ed	$14.95	KWL
Write Your Will (audio cassette), Warner & Greene	1st Ed	$14.95	TWYW
5 Ways to Avoid Probate (audio cassette), Warner & Greene	1st Ed	$14.95	TPRO

GOING TO COURT

Represent Yourself in Court, Bergman & Berman-Barrett	1st Ed	$29.95	RYC
Everybody's Guide to Municipal Court (California), Duncan	1st Ed	$29.95	MUNI
Everybody's Guide to Small Claims Court (California), Warner	11th Ed	$18.95	CSCC
Everybody's Guide to Small Claims Court (National), Warner	5th Ed	$18.95	NSCC
Fight Your Ticket (California), Brown	5th Ed	$18.95	FYT
Collect Your Court Judgment (California), Scott, Elias & Goldoftas	2nd Ed	$19.95	JUDG
How to Change Your Name (California), Loeb & Brown	6th Ed	$24.95	NAME
The Criminal Records Book (California), Siegel	3rd Ed	$19.95	CRIM
Winning in Small Claims Court, Warner & Greene (audio cassette)	1st Ed	$14.95	TWIN

LEGAL REFORM

Fed Up with the Legal System: What's Wrong and How to Fix It, Warner & Elias	2nd Ed	$9.95	LEG

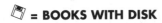 = BOOKS WITH DISK

BUSINESS & WORKPLACE

🖫 Taking Care of Your Corporation, Vol. I:			
Director & Shareholder Meetings Made Easy, Mancuso	1st Ed	$26.95	CORK
🖫 Software Development: A Legal Guide, Fishman	1st Ed	$44.95	SFT
The Legal Guide for Starting & Running a Small Business, Steingold	1st Ed	$22.95	RUNS
Sexual Harassment on the Job, Petrocelli & Repa	1st Ed	$14.95	HARS
Your Rights in the Workplace, Repa	2nd Ed	$15.95	YRW
How to Write a Business Plan, McKeever	4th Ed	$19.95	SBS
Marketing Without Advertising, Phillips & Rasberry	1st Ed	$14.00	MWAD
The Partnership Book, Clifford & Warner	4th Ed	$24.95	PART
The California Nonprofit Corporation Handbook, Mancuso	6th Ed	$29.95	NON
🖫 The California Nonprofit Corporation Handbook, Mancuso	DOS	$39.95	NPI
	MAC	$39.95	NPM
🖫 How to Form a Nonprofit Corporation (National), Mancuso	DOS	$39.95	NNP
How to Form Your Own California Corporation, Mancuso	7th Ed	$29.95	CCOR
🖫 How to Form Your Own California Corporation			
With Corporate Records Binder and Disk, Mancuso	1st Ed	$39.95	CACI
The California Professional Corporation Handbook, Mancuso	5th Ed	$34.95	PROF
🖫 How to Form Your Own Florida Corporation, Mancuso	DOS	$39.95	FLCO
🖫 How to Form Your Own New York Corporation, Mancuso	DOS	$39.95	NYCO
How to Form Your Own Texas Corporation, Mancuso	4th Ed	$29.95	TCOR
How to Form Your Own Texas Corporation, Mancuso	DOS	$39.95	TCI
The Independent Paralegal's Handbook, Warner	3rd Ed	$29.95	PARA
Getting Started as an Independent Paralegal, Warner (audio cassette)	2nd Ed	$44.95	GSIP
How To Start Your Own Business:			
Small Business Law, Warner & Greene (audio cassette)	1st Ed	$14.95	TBUS

THE NEIGHBORHOOD

Neighbor Law: Fences, Trees, Boundaries & Noise, Jordan	1st Ed	$14.95	NEI
Safe Home, Safe Neighborhoods: Stopping Crime Where You Live,			
Mann & Blakeman	1st Ed	$14.95	SAFE
Dog Law, Randolph	2nd Ed	$12.95	DOG

🖫 = BOOKS WITH DISK

MONEY MATTERS

Stand Up to the IRS, Daily	2nd Ed	$21.95	SIRS
Money Troubles: Legal Strategies to Cope With Your Debts, Leonard	2nd Ed	$16.95	MT
How to File for Bankruptcy, Elias, Renauer & Leonard	4th Ed	$25.95	HFB
Simple Contracts for Personal Use, Elias & Stewart	2nd Ed	$16.95	CONT
Nolo's Law Form Kit: Power of Attorney,Clifford, Randolph & Goldoftas	1st Ed	$14.95	KPA
Nolo's Law Form Kit: Personal Bankruptcy, Elias, Renauer, Leonard & Goldoftas	1st Ed	$14.95	KBNK
Nolo's Law Form Kit: Rebuild Your Credit, Leonard & Goldoftas	1st Ed	$14.95	KCRD
Nolo's Law Form Kit: Loan Agreements, Stewart & Goldoftas	1st Ed	$14.95	KLOAN
Nolo's Law Form Kit: Buy & Sell Contracts, Elias, Stewart & Goldoftas	1st Ed	$9.95	KCONT

FAMILY MATTERS

Smart Ways to Save Money During & After Divorce, Collins & Wall	1st Ed	$14.95	SAVMO
How to Raise or Lower Child Support In California, Duncan & Siegel	2nd Ed	$17.95	CHLD
Divorce & Money, Woodhouse & Felton-Collins with Blakeman	2nd Ed	$21.95	DIMO
The Living Together Kit, Ihara & Warner	7th Ed	$24.95	LTK
The Guardianship Book (California), Goldoftas & Brown	1st Ed	$19.95	GB
A Legal Guide for Lesbian and Gay Couples, Curry & Clifford	8th Ed	$24.95	LG
How to Do Your Own Divorce in California, Sherman	19th Ed	$21.95	CDIV
Practical Divorce Solutions, Sherman	1st Ed	$14.95	PDS
California Marriage & Divorce Law, Warner, Ihara & Elias	11th Ed	$19.95	MARR
How to Adopt Your Stepchild in California, Zagone & Randolph	4th Ed	$22.95	ADOP
Nolo's Pocket Guide to Family Law, Leonard & Elias	3rd Ed	$14.95	FLD
Divorce: A New Yorker's Guide to Doing it Yourself, Alexandra	1st Ed	$24.95	NYDIV

JUST FOR FUN

29 Reasons Not to Go to Law School, Warner, Ihara & Repa	4th Ed	$9.95	29R
Devil's Advocates, Roth & Roth	1st Ed	$12.95	DA
Poetic Justice, Roth & Roth	1st Ed	$9.95	PJ

PATENT, COPYRIGHT & TRADEMARK

Trademark: How To Name Your Business & Product, McGrath & Elias, with Shena	1st Ed	$29.95	TRD
Patent It Yourself, Pressman	3rd Ed	$39.95	PAT
The Inventor's Notebook, Grissom & Pressman	1st Ed	$19.95	INOT
The Copyright Handbook, Fishman	2nd Ed	$24.95	COHA

TO ORDER CALL 800-992-6656

LANDLORDS & TENANTS

The Landlord's Law Book, Vol. 1: Rights & Responsibilities (California), Brown & Warner	4th Ed	$32.95	LBRT
The Landlord's Law Book, Vol. 2: Evictions (California), Brown	4th Ed	$32.95	LBEV
Tenants' Rights (California), Moskovitz & Warner	12th Ed	$18.95	CTEN
Nolo's Law Form Kit: Leases & Rental Agreements (California), Warner & Stewart	1st Ed	$14.95	KLEAS

HOMEOWNERS

How to Buy a House in California, Warner, Serkes & Devine.	3rd Ed	$24.95	BHCA
For Sale By Owner, Devine	2nd Ed	$24.95	FSBO
Homestead Your House, Warner, Sherman & Ihara	8th Ed	$9.95	HOME
The Deeds Book, Randolph	2nd Ed	$15.95	DEED

OLDER AMERICANS

Beat the Nursing Home Trap: A Consumer's Guide to Choosing & Financing Long Term Care, Matthews	2nd Ed	$18.95	ELD
Social Security, Medicare & Pensions, Matthews with Berman	5th Ed	$18.95	SOA

RESEARCH/REFERENCE

Legal Research, Elias & Levinkind	3rd Ed	$19.95	LRES
Legal Research Made Easy: A Roadmap Through the Law Library Maze (2 1/2 hr videotape & manual), Nolo & Legal Star	1st Ed	$89.95	LRME

CONSUMER

How to Win Your Personal Injury Claim, Matthews	1st Ed	$24.95	PICL
Nolo's Pocket Guide to California Law, Guerin & Nolo Press Editors	2nd Ed	$10.95	CLAW
Nolo's Pocket Guide to California Law on Disk,	Windows	$24.95	CLWIN
Guerin & Nolo Press Editors	MAC	$24.95	CLM
Nolo's Law Form Kit: Hiring Child Care & Household Help, Repa & Goldoftas	1st Ed	$14.95	KCHLD
Nolo's Pocket Guide to Consumer Rights, Kaufman	2nd Ed	$12.95	CAG

IMMIGRATION

How to Get a Green Card: Legal Ways to Stay in the U.S.A., Lewis with Madlanscay	1st Ed	$22.95	GRN

SOFTWARE

WillMaker 5.0, Nolo Press	Windows	$69.95	WI5
	DOS	$69.95	WI5
	MAC	$69.95	WM5
Nolo's Personal RecordKeeper 3.0, Pladsen & Warner	DOS	$49.95	FRI3
	MAC	$49.95	FRM3
Nolo's Living Trust 1.0, Randolph	MAC	$79.95	LTM1
Nolo's Partnership Maker 1.0, Mancuso & Radtke	DOS	$129.95	PAGI1
California Incorporator 1.0, Mancuso	DOS	$129.00	INCI
Patent It Yourself 1.0, Pressman	Windows	$229.95	PYW1

RECYCLE YOUR OUT-OF-DATE BOOKS AND GET 25% OFF YOUR NEXT PURCHASE

It's important to have the most current legal information. Because laws and legal procedures change often, we update our books regularly. To help keep you up-to-date we are extending this special offer. Cut out and mail the title portion of the cover of any old Nolo book with your next order and we'll give you a 25% discount off the retail price of ANY new Nolo book you purchase directly from us. For current prices and editions call us at 1-800-992-6656. This offer is to individuals only. Prices subject to change.

VISIT OUR STORE

If you live in the Bay Area, be sure to visit the Nolo Press Bookstore on the corner of 9th & Parker Streets in west Berkeley. You'll find our complete line of books and software—all at a discount. CALL 1-510-704-2248 for hours.

ORDER FORM

Code	Quantity	Title	Unit price	Total
			Subtotal	
		California residents add Sales Tax		
	Shipping & Handling ($4 for 1st item; $1 each additional)			
	2nd day UPS (additional $5; $8 in Alaska and Hawaii)			
			TOTAL	

Name _____

Address _____

_____

(UPS to street address, Priority Mail to P.O. boxes)

FOR FASTER SERVICE, USE YOUR CREDIT CARD AND OUR TOLL-FREE NUMBERS

Monday-Friday, 7 a.m. to 6 p.m. Pacific Time

Order Line   1 (800) 992-6656 (in the 510 area code, call 549-1976)

General Information   1 (510) 549-1976

Fax your order   1 (800) 645-0895 (in the 510 area code, call 548-5902)

METHOD OF PAYMENT

☐ Check enclosed

☐ VISA   ☐ MasterCard   ☐ Discover Card   ☐ American Express

Account # _____ Expiration Date _____

Authorizing Signature _____

Daytime Phone _____

Allow 2-3 weeks for delivery. Prices subject to change.

CORK 1.0

NOLO PRESS, 950 PARKER ST., BERKELEY, CA 94710

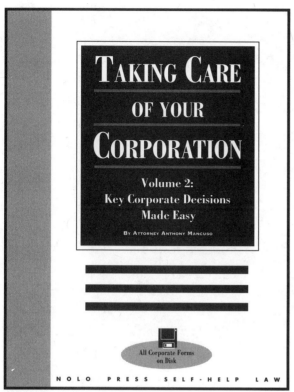

HOW TO FORM YOUR OWN CORPORATION IS ALSO AVAILABLE FOR THESE STATES:

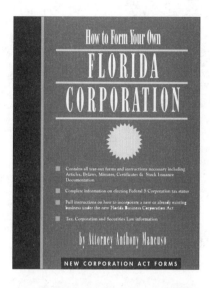

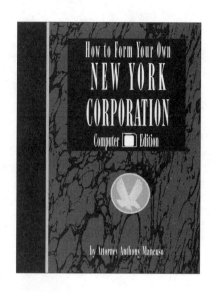

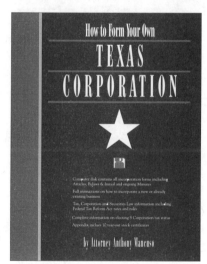

BOOKS WITH FORMS ON DISK & TEAR-OUTS

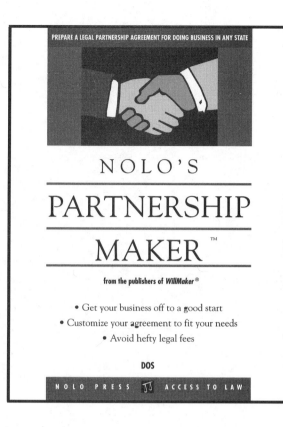

PREPARE A LEGAL PARTNERSHIP AGREEMENT FOR DOING BUSINESS IN ANY STATE

NOLO'S
PARTNERSHIP
MAKER ™

from the publishers of *WillMaker* ®

• Get your business off to a good start
• Customize your agreement to fit your needs
• Avoid hefty legal fees

DOS

NOLO PRESS 🎲 ACCESS TO LAW

CREATE A LEGAL

PARTNERSHIP

AGREEMENT

ON YOUR

COMPUTER

Nolo's Partnership Maker allows you to quickly and easily prepare a legal partnership agreement on your computer. Using the step-by-step legal help, you can select and fill in clauses, print an agreement and show it to your partners for feedback. Repeat the process until you settle on a final agreement. Once you are satisfied, you can print out the agreement and have it signed by all the partners. And, you can change or revise your agreement at any time.

Nolo's Partnership Maker provides:

• 84 standard and alternative clauses
• on-line, step-by-step legal help for understanding each clause and filling in each blank
• an on-line editor that allows for customizing your agreement

Using *Nolo's Partnership Maker*, you and your partners decide:

• who contributes what to the venture
• what happens if a partner fails to contribute agreed upon money or services
• how profits and losses get divided
• how partners will be compensated
• how a partner can sell out or leave the partnership
• how to handle disputes without paying costly legal fees

SYSTEM REQUIREMENTS
Dos 3.0 or higher, 512K Ram.

FREE TECHNICAL SUPPORT
Nolo Press offers free technical support to all registered owners.

UNCONDITIONAL GUARANTEE
All Nolo products have an unconditional guarantee. If for any reason you are unhappy with *Nolo's Partnership Maker*, simply return it to us for a refund.

TO ORDER CALL **1-800-992-6656** OR USE
THE ORDER FORM IN THE BACK OF THE BOOK.

FREE NOLO NEWS SUBSCRIPTION

When you register, we'll send you our quarterly newspaper, the *Nolo News,* free for two years. (U.S. addresses only.) Here's what you'll get in every issue:

INFORMATIVE ARTICLES

Written by Nolo editors, articles provide practical legal information on issues you encounter in everyday life: family law, wills, debts, consumer rights, and much more.

UPDATE SERVICE

The *Nolo News* keeps you informed of legal changes that affect any Nolo book and software program.

BOOK AND SOFTWARE REVIEWS

We're always looking for good legal and consumer books and software from other publishers. When we find them, we review them and offer them in our mail order catalog.

ANSWERS TO YOUR LEGAL QUESTIONS

Our readers are always challenging us with good questions on a variety of legal issues. So in each issue, "Auntie Nolo" gives sage advice and sound information.

COMPLETE NOLO PRESS CATALOG

The *Nolo News* contains an up-to-the-minute catalog of all Nolo books and software, which you can order using our toll-free "800" order line. And you can see at a glance if you're using an out-of-date version of a Nolo product.

LAWYER JOKES

Nolo's famous lawyer joke column continually gets the goat of the legal establishment. If we print a joke you send in, you'll get a $20 Nolo gift certificate.

We promise *never* to give your name and address to any other organization.

Your Registration Card

Complete and Mail Today

Taking Care of Your Corporation, Vol. 1   Registration Card

We'd like to know what you think! Please take a moment to fill out and return this postage paid card for a free two-year subscription to the *Nolo News.* If you already receive the *Nolo News,* we'll extend your subscription.

Name _____ Ph.(   ) _____

Address _____

City _____ State _____ Zip _____

Where did you hear about this book? _____

For what purpose did you use this book? _____

	Yes	No	Not Applicable			
Did you consult a lawyer?	Yes	No	Not Applicable			
Was it easy for you to use this book?	(very easy) 5	4	3	2	1	(very difficult)
Did you find this book helpful?	(very) 5	4	3	2	1	(not at all)

Comments _____
_____
_____
_____
_____
_____

THANK YOU   **CORK 1.0**

[Nolo books are]..."written in plain language, free of legal mumbo jumbo, and spiced with witty personal observations."

—ASSOCIATED PRESS

"Well-produced and slickly written, the [Nolo] books are designed to take the mystery out of seemingly involved procedures, carefully avoiding legalese and leading the reader step-by-step through such everyday legal problems as filling out forms, making up contracts, and even how to behave in court."

—SAN FRANCISCO EXAMINER

"...Nolo publications...guide people simply through the how, when, where and why of law."

—WASHINGTON POST

"Increasingly, people who are not lawyers are performing tasks usually regarded as legal work... And consumers, using books like Nolo's, do routine legal work themselves."

—NEW YORK TIMES

"...All of [Nolo's] books are easy-to-understand, are updated regularly, provide pull-out forms...and are often quite moving in their sense of compassion for the struggles of the lay reader."

—SAN FRANCISCO CHRONICLE

NO POSTAGE
NECESSARY
IF MAILED
IN THE
UNITED STATES

BUSINESS REPLY MAIL
FIRST-CLASS MAIL PERMIT NO 3283 BERKELEY CA

POSTAGE WILL BE PAID BY ADDRESSEE

NOLO PRESS
950 Parker Street
Berkeley CA 94710-9867